PRAISE FOR DYING TO SEE

D1232321

A wonderful testament to the healing journey of Janet D. Tarantino where she establishes a fantastic relationship between her NDE and the spiritual knowledge of the self. It is one of the best NDE books that I have read.

DR. J. VIGNESH SHANKAR, PHD
Psychologist/Author, *The Secret of Mind and Beyond*
Tamil Nadu, India

For readers seeking a detailed first-hand account of three near-death experiences and their aftereffects, interpreted from a Christian perspective yet not limited by the Bible, and addressing the big questions of spirit, meaning, and purpose in life, this book will tantalize and provide much to ponder.

JANICE MINER HOLDEN, EDD, LPC-S, NCC, ACMHP
Retired Professor of Counseling
Past President, International Association for Near-Death Studies
University of North Texas

In Dying to See, *Janet Tarantino shares her deeply personal and spiritual near-death experiences. Janet's Christ-centered experiences gave her life greater context and perspective. Now, in* Dying to See, *she generously and courageously shares what she learned.*

JEFF O'DRISCOLL, MD FACEP
I Exist to Help Souls Heal
Physician, Spiritual Mentor, Speaker, Award-Winning Author, Artist, Healer

Dying to See *is a richly detailed account of three different near-death experiences that unfolded from different perspectives. First, as a young child, she was left wondering what she had witnessed in the clouds, and later as a young mother, given a chance to view future life events and stay to intervene. After seeing what an important role she would play in her son's life, she knew she must return.* Dying to See *bears witness that Janet has another significant role on this earth, and through her eloquent writing, she shares her testimonial of God's unconditional love for each one of us. This book is a warm glimpse into the afterlife and a must-read.*

CLAUDIA WATTS EDGE
Author of the award-winning series: *Gifts from the Edge* and *We Touched Heaven*
NDE and Dream Vision Speaker, Spiritual Mentor, and Hospice Volunteer

After many years of silence, Janet Tarantino courageously steps out of the shadows to reveal her intimate story of not only one but three near-death experiences. In her book Dying to See, *she opens our awareness by lifting the veils of illusion of this 3rd-dimensional reality, helping us see that there is so much more than what meets the eye. If you are new to this phenomenon, you will be fascinated as she takes you on a journey revealing spiritual truths and insights. If you have had your own personal NDE, Janet's story may sound familiar and will validate and permit you to share your own. In these awakening times,* Dying to See *is a valuable beacon for those seeking a broader perspective and a timely reminder that we are all eternal beings of light and the love of One Universal consciousness.*

CARA HOPE CLARK
Bestselling and award-winning author of
*Widow's Moon: A Memoir of Healing,
Hope & Self-Discovery Through Grief & Loss*

We all look for answers and the meaning of life - whether we are ill or have had a loved one pass and suffer from grief. Dying to See *gives us those answers and so much more. We can all live a life of purpose, gratitude, and love, knowing when the final moment comes, we merely close our eyes in this world and reopen them in our natural home in Heaven. Janet Tarantino shares such gems of spiritual wisdom to help us live a great life, plus some great drawings of what she saw on the Other Side. This inspiring and beautifully written book is undoubtedly a gift to the world.*

SANDRA CHAMPLAIN
Author of the #1 International best seller
We Don't Die: A Skeptic's Discovery of Life After Death
Host of *"We Don't Die Radio"*

DYING
to see

Cover Design: Despina Loupeti • Dee Graphic Design • www.deegraphicdesign.com
Print & eBook Design: Dayna Linton • Day Agency • www.dayagency.com

ISBN: 978-1-7340811-1-4 (Paperback)
ISBN: 978-1-7340811-0-7 (eBook)

Library of Congress Number: 2019918409

Printed in the United States of America

10 9 8 7 6 5 4 3 2 1

WELCOME
And thank you for purchasing

DYING
To See

Revelations About God, Jesus, Our Pathways,
And The Nature Of Our Soul

The mortal world is a journey of many souls who should love, lift, and support each other, and I want to invite you to join me on any or all of my social media sites listed below.

I also invite you to check out my website, where you will find helpful information, including a blog about how spirit communicates with us. See you there!

facebook.com/JanetTarantinoNDEr

instagram.com/janettarantino_author

twitter.com/_JanetTarantino

Youtube: bit.ly/3DoXKJP

Website: JanetTarantino.com

Email: JanetTarantinoAuthor@gmail.com

I dedicate this book to the Supreme Source
who tells us in Revelation 22:13:
"I am the Alpha and the Omega, the First and the Last, the Beginning
and the End" (NLT).
Because He really is!

ACKNOWLEDGMENTS

I T HAS BEEN AN incredible privilege to write this book. Without the abiding love of Divine Source and without my heartfelt desire to acknowledge Him, this book would never have come into being. So, I give thanks to the Creator of All for having faith in my writing abilities when I didn't have faith in myself. It was his inspiration that allowed me to describe how he has worked in my life—and in your life, too—that will give others the comfort and knowledge that we never die and we're never alone! Thank you! Thank you! Thank you!

Special thanks to my children, Phillip, Curt, and Gina, who have shown me unfailing love and who stood by me even throughout the strangest of times. And an extra special thank you to my daughter, Gina, for playing such a significant part in my spiritual journey.

A heartfelt thank you goes out to my mom and dad; my brother Dennis and his wife Judy; my brother Doug; and my sister Diane for always being there for me.

My profound gratitude and love go to Bob, who God brought into my life from the other side of the world, not only to love me, but to help me in this life's quest for discovery. His participation allowed me to gain the insight needed for a special life-changing lesson.

Thanks too to James Demos, who set me on a path of discovery by spurring me on to develop my intuitive skills.

A heartfelt thanks to Teresa Dunwell, an extraordinary artist whose intuitive and artistic ability profoundly shook my world when she painted a picture that was a message from Heaven.

I also would like to thank the editors, Michael Ireland, Hannah Lyon, and Sean Linton whose editorial talents and skills helped to organize and bring the reader into the story, so they too could live the experience. Thank you all for sharing your inspirational gifts with the world.

My most profound gratitude goes to the people who read my manuscript and gave me words of encouragement, and to the many others who have helped me in untold ways on my spiritual journey. You all know who you are.

Much love to all,
Janet Tarantino

TABLE OF CONTENTS

FOREWORD

ALTHOUGH I REFER TO God as a male entity the God I know is genderless and can reveal Himself in any form He desires. Since the mid-1970's the studies of near-death experiences have revealed the Creator seems to design each person's experience specifically for the needs of that individual. In my case, my experiences followed the Christian tradition in which I was accustomed to as a child, and some of the Spiritual traditions I have grown accustomed to as an adult, consequently I will honor what He created for me and will describe it in that fashion.

For the purpose of this book I refer to God, Jesus, and the Holy Spirit (also known simply as Spirit) in a personal manner—because they do indeed want to be personal with us.

Also, due to copyright guidelines, some Bible verses that were pertinent appear as required by the publisher. For example, the word "Lord" sometimes appears in phrases within quotation marks in all capital letters, with just the "L" in normal print size. When presented in this fashion, please read "LORD" as the supreme being of love known as God or the Universal Consciousness. All other "Lords" are specified in the text as "Lord God," "Jesus," "Lord Jesus," or "Son of God," depending upon the Bible version used.

1

IT TOOK DYING TO SEE

F IRST OF ALL, YOU might ask, "What is a near-death experience?" According to Bruce Greyson, MD, Professor Emeritus of Psychiatry and Neurobehavioral Sciences at the University of Virginia, a near-death experience (NDE) is a profound psychological event that may occur to a person close to death or, if not near death, in a situation of physical or emotional crisis. Because it includes transcendental and mystical elements, an NDE is a powerful event of consciousness; however, it is not a mental illness.[1]

The mystical elements many people claim to encounter in such an experience appear to be glimpses of eternity. Some of the top reported elements are:

[1] Greyson, B. "Near-Death Experiences." In *Varieties of Anomalous Experiences.* Edited by S.J. Lynn, et al., pp. 315-352. Washington, DC: American Psychological Association, 2000.

- a brilliant white light that appears to be a "being of light"
- a tunnel
- a profound sense of peace and unbound love
- finding yourself outside of your body
- sensing of a border that if you crossed you would not return
- encountering high spiritual beings
- angels
- previously lost loved ones
- a life review

Dr. Bruce Greyson has studied near-death and similar transformative experiences since the mid-1970s. He has defined such experiences, in the 2nd edition of the previously mentioned book, as "complex, life-changing events that are both psychological and physiological." He found that it's not necessary to be in a near-death situation to have such an experience; rather, an NDE or spiritually transformative experience can happen in intense physical and psychological defining moments.[2]

The keywords in Dr. Greyson's description here are *life-changing* and *transformative*. As human consciousness and spirituality author Caroline Myss says in her book *Entering the Castle*, "One needs only the briefest encounter with God . . . to be convinced for the rest of your life that you have been visited by the divine."[3]

---

[2] Greyson, B. "Near-Death Experiences." In *Varieties of Anomalous Experiences*. 2nd ed. Edited by S.J. Lynn, et al., pp. 333-367. Washington, DC: American Psychological Association, 2014.
[3] Myss, C. *Entering the Castle*. New York: Free Press, 2007.

Researchers have also found that it's the recognizable after-effects of having encountered the celestial realm and the experiencer's profound life changes that determine whether or not an event can be called a "near-death experience" or a "spiritually transformative experience." Most notable is the recognizable aftereffect of electrical phenomena surrounding an NDEr that causes electrical malfunctions. Later on, I will tell you more about the amazing aftereffects that happened to me.

You can imagine how confusing it was for me to understand the depth and complexity of these life-altering spiritual events. To be honest with you, I kept all of these unusual experiences to myself, either discounting them in some fashion or not telling anyone. Who could I tell that would believe me? Not to mention I had trouble making sense of them for quite some time because I had never heard of such things.

After the third NDE, I received a message from the heavenly voice of God to share my experiences in this book, so I started planning the manuscript's creation. I also started sharing my experiences in one-on-one situations when the opportunities presented themselves. Amazingly, unlike the initial negative responses received from my first attempts to share my story, people found comfort, hope, and peace in knowing the fact that we never die, and that God has unfailing and unconditional love for everyone. It is also comforting for people to understand that God provides us with immeasurable divine guidance—not only inside of us but around us at all times.

In this book, I describe my near-death experiences (NDEs) and spiritually transformative experiences (STEs) in detail, and provide references to passages in the Bible to help you understand the spiritual significance of these experiences. For much of my life, I had no idea that these things were in the Bible, but after my third miraculous NDE (which was more spiritually intense than the others), I decided it was time to read scripture. I found so many verses that referred to what I saw or experienced during my NDEs that I saw the Bible in a new light. I also saw that my separate experiences were tied together and built upon each other to create a bigger picture, which you will no doubt see, as well.

I was brought up as a Christian, so I often refer to the super spiritual power as God, but as I grew into adulthood, I also knew Him as Oneness, the Universal Consciousness, the Supreme Creator, Love, the I AM, Mr. Wonderful or many other names. But the God I know is much bigger than just a supreme being—He is the very fabric of existence. He is the one, universal consciousness that we are joined with on this mortal plane of existence and on a much higher level of awareness beyond the veil that separates this realm from eternity. After years of silence regarding my three near-death experiences (NDEs) and other spiritually transformative experiences (STEs), I'm ready to share what happened and what I've learned.

Because these spiritual experiences were both powerful and profound, friends have often asked me why I stayed silent so long. My answer was always: "It just wasn't the right time."

Now, people all over the world are sharing the intimate details of their near-death and spiritually transformative experiences. Those of us who have had these experiences are standing up, reassuring the world that the Superior Creator is real, and that even though our physical bodies may succumb to the natural order of earthly existence, our spirits live an eternal life—just as the Holy Bible and other sacred texts describe. I can attest to this personally because, during my NDEs, I felt more alive than I felt in this world, I continued to retain the thoughts and memories of the person I was in the mortal world, and in the heavenly realm I saw God, Jesus, the Holy Spirit, and other divine helpers.

What was revealed to me is that God orchestrates events in our lives at just the right time. God showed me this through a mind to mind consciousness connection during my most profound near-death experience. As the combining of our minds occurred, I received an instantaneous download of information and a flashing of cinematic-like visions. After fifteen years of sorting through this knowledge and years of studying NDEs, I finally understand all—or at least most of—what God revealed. He showed me that not only was He always with me, orchestrating events in my life to guide and protect me, but He was guiding and protecting my loved ones, as well.

This is not so inconceivable if you consider God knows everything, as it says in Psalm 139: 2-5: "You know when I sit down and when I get up. You know my thoughts before I think them. You know where I go and where I lie down. You know thoroughly everything I do. LORD, even before I say a word you already know it. You are all around me—in front and in the back—and have put your hand on me" (NCV).

Knowing this truth, as it says in scripture, and the fact that the Supreme Light has incredible strength and abilities far beyond what the human mind can conceive, it is not hard to understand that our lives, or at least specific events of our lives, are recorded before we are born.

I hope that after you read my story, you will recognize the same works of the Divine in your life as He worked in mine, and that it may reassure and strengthen your certainty in the fact that we are eternal beings who transcend death only to return to our real home in heaven.

I am pleased to invite you to come with me, as I share with you the visionary moments God showed to me during my most intense NDE, and get personal with the spiritual beings from the heavenly realm that are there for each of us. He wanted me to know that these moments were specific points in my life that were prearranged and recorded in the celestial record.

Now, LET's TURN THE clock back in time to a visionary moment when I was a little girl. Before the NDEs, I believed there was a higher power but I didn't dwell on it, and after attending school all week, I didn't want to attend school again on Sunday. I was a kid, after all, and I wanted to go jump rope or ice skating. Anywhere outside in nature would be more to my liking. I guess you could say that that was my own version of communing with the Creator. Finally, my two brothers and I whined enough until my mom and dad surrendered, let us stay home, and off they went on Sundays with baby Diane in tow. I was too young and interested in my own world to be thoughtful about a higher world. The earthly world was where the action was, so this realm is what captured my attention.

My spiritual escapades began as a child when, for some reason, I knew things about my life that I shouldn't have known. When I was not yet old enough to go to school, I always waited for my two older brothers and my friend who lived next door to get home in the afternoons. My mom was having a conversation on the telephone with another mom, who was talking about adoption.

When she hung up the phone, I asked her curiously, "Am I adopted?"

"No, silly!" My mom replied right away. "You're our little girl."

That answer satisfied my inquiry, but the next thing out of my mouth were words I will never forget. I told my mom, "Well, okay, but I'm going to die young."

My mom's face immediately shifted to a shocked expression. "Quit talking like that!" she demanded unhappily.

As I stood there looking at my mom's disapproving expression, my little mind contemplated what "young" meant, and visions of different ages flashed through my mind. What I didn't know at the time was that the images I saw were of me at the ages I was to later experience each of my three NDEs.

Such precognitive experiences are referred to in the Bible text of Jeremiah 1:11-19, when God showed Jeremiah glimpses of future events. God didn't say these coming events might happen; on the contrary, He said the occasions will undoubtedly come to pass. The second vision shown to Jeremiah was of a future event of a disaster that will come. How could this be, unless they were already scheduled?

Other little precognitive spiritual experiences happened to me from time to time, but they seemed perfectly reasonable to me, as if they were a routine part of life. Decades later, as I set up a timeline of these visionary moments, a broader picture of my life emerged during my most profound NDE, which led to the planning of this book. I realized that those visions I'd foreseen, such as those I saw before kindergarten, were scheduled. Young Janet, then known as "Jan," hadn't just been gifted with a series of snapshots of her life-to-come—she'd seen pages in her own Book of Life. After all, how could she have known of these experiences if they weren't already planned?

What, you might ask, is The Book of Life? First, The Book of Life contains the knowledge acquired from paths recorded in the heavenly record of all eternity. The heavenly record of all eternity is the recording of everything, including all thoughts, actions, and all that we've ever said, from not only the past, but the present, and future too. It also contains our regrets, heartaches, and humiliations that are yet to be overcome. In essence, all those moments where we felt we could do better are included. The Book of Life is this life's ingenious storyline that will bring us to a deeper understanding of what we're here to overcome, experience and learn from. But not only should we learn—we must implement those learnings and overcome negative Karma from previously harmful moments.

It took me finding out what an NDE is (and all that an NDE entails) to understand the meaning of my younger self's precognitive visions. As it turned out, my NDEs were so transformative that I went from being called "Jan" to "Janet" because that name suited the different, new, and improved person I had become.

2

MY FIRST NDE
The Sumo Wrestler and
Music Box Lady

T HE YEAR OF MY transition from middle school to high
school arrived, and while I didn't yet know it, I would
soon have a most unusual experience. Our family lived
across the street from a golf course and park. The grounds consisted of the golf green and fairway, a playground with swings
and toys, a picnic area, tennis courts, and a big swimming pool.

My mom babysat some of my cousins during the summers—
we kids loved having playmates. We always planned our day's
activities together and often went golfing. When we did, our
cousins would come prepared, golf clubs in tow, and with what
they brought and the ones available at our house, we had enough
to share. We headed out the door in the morning, the screen door

slamming behind us, anxious to see how we'd score that day. The sun just came up, with dewdrops still glistening on the grass.

A couple of houses up the street was the end of the fifth hole and the teeing area to the sixth. The clubhouse was located on the other side of the course, so, often—if there weren't any other golfers yet—we'd tee-off on the sixth hole instead of walking all the way around the course. Pretty smart, huh? We took turns teeing off, and played up to the golf course clubhouse, where we'd pay our green fees. Then we began again from the clubhouse and played the course back home, making it a total of nine holes.

In the afternoons—when we weren't golfing—us kids trekked excitedly, towels in hand, to the swimming pool. Fortunately, the golf course was lined with big elm trees that protected the houses and the people who walked by from flying golf balls, but there were no guarantees. My mom always warned us to watch out for stray balls—it wasn't uncommon for a ball to end up in someone's front yard. So while we walked, we kept an eye out for errant balls that might come soaring our way.

My cousins and I were eager to get to the pool because we wanted to be among the first swimmers to arrive. Hanging out at the pool was a favorite pastime for both children and adults, and the payment queue grew fast, especially in extreme heat. If we got in line early enough, we could claim the prime spots to lay our towels. The pool had a concession stand, and during breaks, we bought a treat. My personal favorites were Fudgsicles® and BIG HUNK® bars.

During a few summers leading up to my high school years, we earned a bit of money working. My brother Dennis found a job detasseling corn and asked my other brother Doug, my two cousins, and I if we wanted to do it, too. The job involved walking in rows of cornfields and picking tassels off designated rows before the corn tasseled out and pollinated. It was, I know now, an early method of genetically modifying corn.

Our parents said we could take the job and asked what we planned to use our money for. That summer I had just finished middle school and told my parents I'd be buying clothes for my first year of high school. It was a new school in a new location, and I was looking forward to the "big time" with all the student activities and dances—not to mention the dating life. I was interested in fashion and couldn't wait to wear my new outfits to school, compliments of my corn-detasseling money.

Each year, the high school had orientation day about a week before the school year started, to allow new students to get acquainted with the layout of the school, meet their teachers, and get to know each other. The students were to meet in their assigned homeroom class, where the teacher distributed class schedules and locker numbers. The students were then enlightened with the rules, given time to find classrooms, and encouraged to introduce themselves to the teachers if they wanted. It was going to be an exciting event that would put everyone at ease for the start of the year.

I didn't get to go to orientation day because I fell ill.

A few days prior, our extended family had one last family picnic before school started in our favorite park some distance away from home. It was an all-day affair. The day was hot and sunny, and we were fortunate to get some tables where the trees provided shade. Within a matter of days after that picnic, however, I started feeling queasy and couldn't stop throwing up.

I was violently ill. When my illness didn't subside, my mom decided to remove my little sister from the bedroom we shared so my mom could sleep with me and take care of me. Diane, who is five years younger than I, was delighted she got to sleep with my dad, so she happily hopped into bed with him. I was comforted knowing my mom was going to be beside me.

The following days I got worse and could only lay limp in bed in between scrambling back and forth to the bathroom.

One night, my mom and I fell asleep. Sometime during the nighttime, I woke up feeling like death warmed over. I looked up at the ceiling, with my mouth watering and my stomach rolling yet again. I could smell the putrid, sweet but sour smell of sweat, sickness and the edges of death. My hearing was muffled with a strange ringing vibration as if I was listening from outside this dimension. Unexpectedly, my eyes rolled up into my head. Even though I was laying down, I felt like I had lost my balance and suddenly had the strange feeling that I'd fallen out of my body.

I blinked, until I was able to see above me again, and I noticed a swirling motion on the ceiling. The light fixture over my head twirled to the right like the hands of a clock, and all of a sudden the ceiling turned into a sky of clouds. It all happened so quickly—I didn't have time to be concerned. My head tilted, my gaze became blank, and my mouth gaped open, entranced with the unworldly transformation above me.

There was another spinning motion, in two separate areas of the clouds overhead, which swiftly opened to show me another world.

My gaze curiously darted between the two holes while they rotated to a lower position (or I floated to a higher position, I don't know). I only know the holes were now in front and slightly above me, instead of far above me on the ceiling's surface. *Whoa,* I thought. *What's going on?* The openings had depth to them, and I watched in interest as separate tunnels formed through the banks of clouds.

I thought, *If I run fast enough, like I have in track and field, I could easily jump the five to seven feet between me and that other world at the end of the tunnel in front of me.* I wanted to, but for some odd reason something kept me from doing so.

My attention went first to the hole that appeared to the left of where the ceiling light used to be. What I saw there confused me, but I wasn't afraid. Who would have thought I would see a sumo wrestler looking down at me? I know it's strange, but that's what I saw. He was in the distance, sitting at a small, round table.

In the next moment, he stood and walked around the white table and its chair, moving very fast as he watched me. If his eyes diverted at all, they returned to me quickly. His motions were like a film on fast-forward. As I watched this sumo, I noticed he was standing in a radiant light within a white room. His garb was white, and he wore his hair in a topknot. He watched me silently.

Next, my attention went to the opening that had appeared to the right. At that moment the sumo was quickly forgotten when I saw the most mesmerizing, beautiful young woman, with long, thick, almost black hair, sweep down into the opening. Unlike the sumo wrestler, her movements were normal and I heard glorious, heavenly music that she seemed to ride in on.

At the time, I didn't interpret the music as coming from Heaven. I was too young to make that connection, but I know it now. Initially, I thought of her as "daddy's little girl" and "music box lady" because of her beauty and the divine music that accompanied her. These were the only things I could associate the vision with at that point in my life.

The music box lady wore a divinely inspired white gown with a full skirt, like that of a princess. The bottom of her dress had rows of beautiful, layered lace. She swished into view from the upper right of the hole as the music played. Initially, she faced me, but I was so fascinated with her lace dress, I didn't look at her face. She turned, so she was facing the other tunnel. Now her profile faced me, and I knew she was having a conversation with the sumo wrestler, who was still watching me through the other tunnel.

I was infatuated with the princess-like quality of her dress. All my fashion sense was on high alert—the lace on the dress was stunning and I wanted to get a closer look. With that thought, I instantly became an energetic being of consciousness, excitedly zooming in on the intricate lace so I could look through the eyelets as if they were enormous caverns.

I moved, or rather flowed, around the delicate gown. I felt like my eyes were open wide with a sense of awe as I admired the intricacies before me. The threads framing the eyes in the lace were the size of bamboo stalks and held designs of their own. Each eyelet opening appeared to be a cavern in and of itself. I felt like a downhill skier with my windblown hair trailing behind me, weaving around the various obstacles. Instead of flying down a mountainside, I was weaving in and out of the cavernous eyelets of the exquisite dress fit for a princess, twirling atop a music box.

Figure 1 Sumo wrestler and music box lady I saw during my first NDE.

After interweaving myself through the lacy loops, I retreated toward my physical body. The lady moved farther away, higher and higher, and I didn't want her to go. I remember thinking she was being "placed on a pedestal by her daddy."

The room my mom and I were sleeping in was in the front corner of the house. The room had two windows: one on the front of the house, which faced the golf course, and one on the adjacent wall. The headboard was under the window overlooking the golf course.

After I'd zoomed in on the beautiful lady's lace dress, I returned to my physical body, or at least, I thought I did. I perceived myself to be about a foot or two above my physical body. From my vantage point, I floated to the height of the window, two feet above the bed.

I was ecstatic when I realized that while I was out of my body, I was no longer sick. I was filled with a sense of perfection, a fearless freedom, and a sacred peacefulness that's hard to explain. The queasiness went away and I felt spectacular, not to mention the wonderful sense to see flawlessly. I learned that we are whole again once the spiritual body leaves the physical body.

I also noticed that even though all of this was happening in the middle of the night, and the ceiling fixture was switched off, I was surrounded by a comforting and loving light. The room was lit with a soft, white ethereal glow. The spirit beings were clear and standing in a glimmering light. The only darkness was outside the room, even though the ceiling light was not on and it was the middle of the night.

I floated above my physical body as the beautiful lady moved upwards, to where I thought her daddy was placing her on a pedestal. My attention went back to the angelic sumo wrestler. He continued to watch me until the music box lady swished back into view, facing him once more in conversation.

Suddenly, their talk was over, the clouds closed up, and the two beings supernaturally transformed into glowing orbs of light. They flew through me or around me. I didn't know, but suddenly they were behind me on the inside of the room. I didn't have to move physically to see the orbs, because I found

I could see in every direction without moving. My mere intention to look in one direction or another made it so.

As I watched these orbs of light, they felt like friends I knew. I also realized what was happening was natural. I waited for them to communicate with me, but they never did. They danced back and forth as if they were still conversing with one another. I knew they were discussing me and watching me.

The two orbs darted out the front wall facing the golf course. I watched them as they whipped around the outside of the house, as though I had x-ray vision. They paused in the adjacent window, watching me and conversing again. These spheres of light turned to talk to one another, then turned back toward me again. The first orb darted away, leaving the other to monitor me. It returned not long after. Then they both flew along the side of the house and were gone.

I didn't want the orbs to leave. I waited, hoping they'd return. They hadn't communicated anything to me. After a while, I knew they wouldn't be back. That's when I settled back into my body and immediately ran to the bathroom to throw up.

AFTER THIS EVENT, I didn't understand what had happened. I was fearful. Still terribly sick, I lay in bed not eating or drinking so I wouldn't have to throw up again. I could feel, especially at night, that someone was hovering above me, but I couldn't see them. I kept looking at the ceiling to see if the presence I felt with my senses would appear, but it did not.

My mom became very concerned when the illness lasted much longer than a normal bout of flu, so she took me to our family doctor. The doctor examined me and at the end of the appointment, unlike any other of my prior appointments, he very caringly asked me to wait in the waiting room while he talked with my mom. On our way home, mom told me the doctor said I needed to drink fluids, so we stopped for a chocolate milkshake.

Later that evening, I overheard my mom and dad's conversation about the appointment. My mom went on to tell my dad that I was severely dehydrated and the doctor told her I could have died. She was instructed to get fluids into my body as soon as possible, and that must have been why she encouraged me to have a milkshake.

I also remember the following week overhearing my mom tell my dad that she heard on the news that E. coli was found in the water at the park where we had our picnic the weekend before I got sick. Could that have been why I was so ill? I don't remember specifically if I played in the shallow water, but it was a hot day and I loved water. Nonetheless, I will never know for sure.

As I started to recover from my illness, I stayed up all night, trying to sleep during the day because I was afraid. I was frightened because I continued to feel a presence around me, but couldn't see what it was.

All these images were so clear and real that I can still to this day recall the sensations I experienced. When I was a child, I wore glasses with strong prescription lenses, since I had terrible vision. Without my glasses, I could only see colors and vague shapes. I always set my glasses on the nightstand before going to sleep so I could reach them each morning, otherwise, I wouldn't have found them when I woke up.

After reflecting on this event, I realized that to have zoomed up to the gown to inspect it and fly through the lace, I had to have been out-of-body (OBE). In this state of being, as an energetic life force, I had the capability to become small enough to scrutinize the dress as I described. Also, while I was watching the sumo and the music box lady, I could see flawlessly, even though I wasn't wearing my glasses. I could perceive what was behind me as well as in front of me. Lastly, I realized the sumo's initial fast movements were due to us being in different dimensions. But once I was in the same dimension of timelessness, his movements became normal.

As CHILDREN, AND EVEN as adults, we are fearful of what we don't understand. This can be more frightening if what we hear or see has no reference in our corporeal reality to help make sense of it. I believe this is a trait of the human ego. Typically, the ego is defined as the part of our personality that responds to the physical and social world around us and is thought to remember, plan, and evaluate our responses.

This is partially true, but in my opinion, it is the soul that knows all that is true and accurate, and houses our memories and consciousness. The ego taps into the spiritual consciousness and, based on its own personality traits, it is allowed free will to make its own decisions. This includes, of course, our daily choices, as well as situations we don't immediately understand.

The ego often responds with negativity when something can't be readily explained. It doesn't say, "I don't get it, but it must be okay." Instead, it errs habitually on the side of fear, more ready to believe doomsday is coming rather than the sacred affirmations of God sent from Heaven. In other situations, it is the ego that decides to respond to our earthly desires rather than to listen to the guidance of the soul. This is why our ego is sometimes known to "edge God out."

I never told anyone about this event. I thought I'd just been delirious. However, after my last NDE, God gave me an unquenchable thirst for wanting to understand the near-death experience. I was curious and started researching all aspects of the phenomena. In the revelation of unfolding information, I came to recognize that the angelic sumo wrestler was a guide God gave to watch, help, and protect me.

This type of celestial observer is also referred to as a watcher in some Bible versions. It is spoken about in Daniel 4:13: "As I was looking at those things in the vision while lying on my bed, I saw an observer, a holy angel coming down from heaven" (NCV). These types of angels are called observers or watchers because their prime responsibility is to serve, protect, and guide.

This was also confirmed many years later. During my research of telepathic communication, like the occurrences in the later NDEs, I was interested to find out if psychics similarly receive their communication telepathically. I was led to psychic medium James Demos, whose specialty at that time was connecting people with their celestial observer. When James described mine, he described a sumo wrestler with a topknot in his hair. He said he did not see this warrior type of angelic observer guide often. "You must have really needed some protection!" James told me.

I gasped and told James, "I saw him when I was young! I saw a sumo wrestler with his hair in a topknot!" James expressed how my guide had known this meeting was going to happen, and that he'd dressed up in uniform for our formal introduction. My guide said I could refer to him as Fung, since I would never be able to articulate what he was really called.

I found out later who the beautiful lady was too: she's my daughter, Gina, who wouldn't be conceived and born until over fifteen years later. One day, about a year after I'd drawn a picture of the tunnel-cloud scene to record my memory of the sumo wrestler and the music-box-lady, I was visiting my parents. I walked into their kitchen and glanced up at a photo of Gina they had taped to their refrigerator.

This picture was not one I had at my home. I looked at it, trying to figure out where I'd seen the image before. Part of me was telling myself in those moments, "Of course you know her: she's your daughter!" But nevertheless, I was puzzled because I knew it also reminded me of something else. Then, BAM! the fireworks started exploding in my head. I made the connection: the music box lady! Gina had been photographed in a manner, and from that angle I knew unquestionably she was the music box princess. She had a similar facial shape and the same hair. I realized that that was why, at fifteen, I'd thought of the music box lady as "Daddy's little girl."

Figure 2 (On Left) The music box lady from first NDE.

Figure 3 (On Right) My daughter Gina who wasn't even conceived until fifteen years later.

I have no doubt that Gina's spirit wanted to be born at a designated time in the future, and she couldn't have come into this world if I'd died that night. That is why the music box lady (Gina) had appeared—and that was the conversation Gina and my angelic guide had been having. At some level, I believe I was included in the discussion between Gina and my guide and that is why I thought of her as "Daddy's little girl," but I was not allowed to retain that memory. It likely wouldn't have been for the better to remember such a conversation.

Had I remembered the conversation, for example, I may have searched consciously for the correct person to father my child. With each man I met, I might always have wondered: *Is this the father of my daughter?* The fact that my daughter appeared to me on that night is yet more proof that certain features of our lives are predetermined if we stay on the same pathway God has determined for us.

As it is written in Psalm 139:15-16: "You saw my bones being formed as I took shape in my mother's body. When I was put together there, you saw my body as it was formed. All the days planned for me were written in your book before I was one day old" (NCV).

It is also interesting to know the preplanning is referred to in the Bible when Jesus foretells that one of the apostles will betray Him. The apostles were sad and each one of them denied it would be them, but Jesus counters their denials and references the preplanned life in Mark 14:27: "Then Jesus told the followers, 'You will all stumble in your faith, because it is written in the Scriptures'" (NCV).

The pieces of this NDE started to fall into place just a few years ago when I was drawn to read P.M.H. Atwater's books. I read *The New Children and Near-Death Experiences* about the near-death experiences of both adults and children.[4] P.M.H. Atwater, L.H.D., Ph.D. (Hon), mentions that children's NDEs differ from adults' because children explain their experience in terms they are familiar with at their age.

It is easiest, she says, to understand what children are trying to describe by having them draw a picture. She gives an example of a child who, when asked to draw a picture of what he saw, scratched some parallel lines. Between the lines, he drew wobbly lines. He added a circle or two, and a face. When he explained what he drew, he told Atwater it was a ladder to another dimension. She was astounded that he even knew what a dimension was.[5]

---

[4] Atwater, P. *The New Children and Near-Death Experiences*. Rochester, VM: Bear & Company, 2003. E-book.
[5] Atwater, P. *The New Children and Near-Death Experiences*. Rochester, VM: Bear & Company, 2003. E-book, pp. 224-227.

I realized after reading Atwater's books that the unusual experience I'd had at fifteen was my first NDE. I've never forgotten it, which is typical of a near-death experience. It's always as if it happened yesterday, and this was unquestionably the case for me. At fifteen, I didn't dwell on it, and again, that is also common for children.

If you are with a child who is trying to explain something unusual, learn to be silent while you listen. That is key to hearing what a child (or any person) is saying. Notice that although the words "silent" and "listen" both contain the same letters (but in a different order), the two words are deeply connected.

You can't listen if you're not silent, and if you shut a child down when they are trying to communicate with you, they may become frustrated, and that precious communication will end. Imagine how you would feel as a child, and even as an adult, when the one you trusted to share intimate details with became dismissive. Would you trust baring your heart to them again?

What does a near-death or spiritual experience mean to a child? Ms. Atwater explains that most children don't integrate their experiences but instead shelve them or tuck them away and adjust.[6] Ms. Atwater gave some excellent advice about helping children convey what they've experienced, and her words of wisdom about having a child draw a picture are superb. Pictures speak louder than words.

Atwater's conclusions about how children usually shelve their experiences are accurate for me. Even though I long remembered my NDE, I started putting the event behind me as much as I could. I'd convinced myself back then that "it was

---

[6] Atwater, P. *Dying to Know You*. Faber, VA: Rainbow Ridge Book LLC, 2014. E-book.

just a real, technicolor dream." I was fifteen—far more interested in dating than in dreaming—so I tucked it into a safe pocket in my mind. The memory was never forgotten, but it was never shared, either . . . until now.

My mom never knew about the incident, but there was nothing she could have done to prevent it from happening. Even though she was lying beside me, she couldn't see what I was seeing. These kinds of occurrences are silent, invisible to those around us.

My first near-death experience means so much more to me now that I understand on a deeper level what happened that night. My NDE research has helped me to put the puzzle pieces of my life together. I can say for sure that I'm seeing more clearly now. I won't say I have the total picture yet because, throughout one's lifetime, more and more makes sense as life and time evolve.

3
MY SECOND NDE
Divine Intervention

MY LIFE TOOK A sharp turn sideways when I was thirty-eight years old and living in Denver, Colorado. My first husband, Fred and I, had parted ways. We had been married for thirteen years and had three beautiful children: Phillip, Curt, and Gina. Fred and I remain friends to this day as an extended family. Fortunately, I had a great job with a major American corporation, and my position, with its generous paycheck, allowed me to rent a comfortable, three-bedroom home. We had a large, wood backyard deck where we enjoyed barbecuing on summer evenings when it wasn't unbearably hot. Every year, I planted many flower pots brimming with colorful blooms and placed them on the deck for the family to enjoy.

One summer, my son Curt, then in his early teens, touched my heart when he surprised me with a gift he built himself—a beautiful wooden planter that was long enough to frame one edge of the patio. This gift took thinking, planning and the intention to complete, which he certainly succeeded in doing. To me it was an accomplishment of love that I will keep in my heart into eternity.

Our home was in a friendly neighborhood, only two blocks from the local elementary school and a short walk to both the middle school and high school that the children would be attending. The location was perfect. The neighborhood was full of children the same age as my children, and the kids made lots of friends.

My goal was to provide a stable, healthy home for my kids, and to make sure they had a loving and supportive childhood. My own paternal family and siblings lived in Boise, Idaho—over 800 miles away. I could have moved there to be closer to my family, but I didn't want to take the children away from the convenient access to their dad.

During my early days as a single mom in Colorado, I got my life settled, but because I was virtually on my own like many other young parents, I had my hands full. I juggled parenthood, work, and whatever social life I managed to fit in.

Thankfully, I had the moral support of my loving and helpful parents. I talked with them often, especially when my mom called to see how everything was going. One day, my mom and dad offered to take the kids for a month to spend some quality time with their grandchildren. Wow! How awesome was that?

The only thing I needed to do was get the children to them. They planned to have fun with the kids for a few weeks in Boise before taking a road trip to Disneyland in California. After experiencing that magical wonderland, they planned to drive back to Colorado to deliver the children home.

My parents were always conscientious about annual vacations while we were children. They took all of us kids on vacation every summer to open our eyes to what the world had to offer. During those years, we lived in Iowa, and we drove long distances in many directions to experience America. The merry outings included camping trips, and a cross-country drive to various locations like Estes Park, a little, well known resort town close to the Rocky Mountain National Park that was home to the luxurious Stanley Hotel built by the inventor of the Stanley Steamer car.

We made trips through Arizona, too. One year, we were treated to an extra adventure when our car overheated on the outskirts of a small town. My parents took us through Yellowstone National Park and up to Mount Rushmore to see the sculptures and the Black Hills. We saw the majestic Redwood Forest in California, and we swam in the Pacific Ocean (which was freezing!). I could go on, but you get the idea of how grand our parents were in sharing the world with all of us. That couldn't have been easy, especially with six of us in a car without air conditioning.

My parents wanted to share the same kinds of experiences with their grandchildren, so they too could visit Disneyland just as we had. I was thrilled because, as a single mom I wouldn't have been able to treat my three kids to a Disneyland holiday while juggling the responsibilities of my job, the kids' school, and parenting.

I was also delighted that I'd have a little time to rest. A single parent's job is demanding, and long-distance vacations are not usually possible.

When the time came, I took some vacation days from work so I could make the twelve-hour drive to Idaho. Road trip! I wanted to make the trip fun for all of us.

We bought some coloring books, and Fred showed up with some cute travel packages for the kids to enjoy in the car. Even though Fred lived in a different city about an hour away, he always made an effort to spend time with his treasured kids and to contribute in special ways.

We stayed overnight in Ogden, Utah and on the afternoon of the second day of our trip, we pulled into my parent's driveway. The kids were instantly wrapped in Grandma and Grandpa's arms. My brother Doug was there to greet us and later my sister, Diane, and niece Kayla came up as well. It was so great to see everyone—all the fatigue and boredom from the long drive evaporated. The kids settled in, and I heard about all my mom and dad's exciting plans.

I stayed in Boise for a couple of days, then headed back to Denver early one morning, so I could have a few days on my own before I had to return to work on Monday. All on my own now, there was nothing to do except drive, so I ended up making the whole trip in one day. I made it home around eight in the evening. It was funny, getting back to a place where there was usually so much activity. I was alone then, and everything was quiet. It was kind of lonely. I walked down the hallway, looking into my children's empty bedrooms, missing the chatter of their voices and the flurry of activity that was always around them. I settled in, unwound, and headed to bed.

The next morning, after a night of restful sleep, the sun was out in all its glory, the sky was blue, and the weather was mild—a perfect time to go flower shopping. I looked at the planters on the deck, and they were screaming for flowers! I had visions of the pots overflowing with cascading flowers and beautiful vines that we could enjoy each time we had an evening barbecue.

I headed out the door to first stop for a cup of coffee with my friend Gavin. Afterward, I hopped back in the car and headed to a local nursery. *This is going to be a fun day!* I thought.

As expected, the flower nursery had what I wanted. Deciding what colors to decorate with was so much fun. I carried all my treasures to the car to load them in. I drove a Corsica hatchback, so it was easy to load groceries and other items. I opened the hatchback and set the colorful flowers inside. I went down my checklist mentally. Potting soil? Check. Fertilizer? Check. Supplies? Check. I had it all.

I exited the parking lot with the sweet-smelling scents of rich soil and fragrant flowers in my nose, enthusiastic about my purchases and eager to garden my little heart out, not realizing my life was about to change forever.

I scanned the three traffic lanes going in each direction, and the way I was headed had no traffic coming for quite some distance. I leisurely turned right into the outside lane, heading south, then switched into the middle lane. The light just ahead turned red, so I slowed to a stop and passed the time listening to the relaxing music of the radio's easy listening channel. After a short time, the traffic light cycled to green, and I looked in each direction before proceeding through the intersection.

There was almost no traffic in the vicinity, other than the cars I saw when I left the flower nursery, and they were far enough away that I wasn't bothered by them. There was one vehicle going in the opposite direction when the light had changed, but it was of no concern to me.

After the intersection, the road took a dip and there was a sort of blind spot until I descended the hill. I noticed I seemed to be catching up to a vehicle heading in the same direction faster than I should be, even though I wasn't speeding. I realized the car I was approaching had stopped for some unknown reason.

The car before me was not stopped at an intersection, but sat at a standstill at the bottom of the hill in the middle lane (the same lane I was in). I analyzed the situation. *There's a park on the left and an overgrown gully on right. Why is he stopped? Did a child chase a ball into the street? There's a vacant lane to the left and right of the car. If there's a child in front of it, which way would it be going?*

There's no rush, I thought to myself. *I need to stop. I couldn't live with myself if I hurt someone.* I eased on the brake pedal until my car halted.

I glanced in my rearview mirror. All the cars that had been behind me in the distance were now catching up. They crested the hill and sped down it, lined up like race contestants approaching a finish line. Directly behind me, a man in a pickup truck was looking distractedly to his right, and he wasn't slowing down. I knew he didn't see that we were all stopped.

Every car was lined up down the hill, nose-to-nose like horses on a race track. All the lanes were full, so no one could deviate from the lane they were in. They were coming alarmingly fast, and fear rose in my stomach when I realized the situation was critical. *He can't possibly stop in time!* I thought frantically. *He can't go around me! Oh my God, he's going to hit me!*

Now wide-eyed, my mind analyzed the situation at the speed of light: *I haven't bothered to buckle my seat belt. Home is a couple of miles away. I've only traveled a couple of blocks from the nursery. If I fumble with the belt now, I'll end up with my face smashed into the steering wheel, or I might be thrown through the windshield. My car will crumple against the car in front of me. I'll be crushed.*

All of a sudden, I heard a voice say: "Lie down across the seat and cover your face."

I was alone. Who was speaking? Everything was happening so fast, so I did what I was told. *At least my face won't be smashed into the steering wheel.* Because they were not required in those days, I did not have an airbag.

I kept my foot on the brake and lay across the passenger seat. I covered my face with my arms and felt the first impact. Even though I learned later that the force of the collision was tremendous, what I felt in the moment was soft and gentle, like someone bumping into my bed while I slept.

I opened my eyes. In slow motion, the window above me shattered into tiny pieces. The cracks formed gracefully, in a wavelike motion. It was beautiful, as if I was watching the creation of an exquisite piece of art. What I didn't realize was that I was watching the rear hatchback window blow apart.

On impact, my body forced the front seats backward, and I now lay in the back seat. My arms still covered my face, and I closed my eyes again quickly against the rain of glass.

I felt the second impact then, and it too felt like a minor bump. *That wasn't so bad,* I thought. Then all of a sudden my body was lifted into the air. Instead of being thrown forward through the windshield or being smashed into the dashboard, I felt an enormous arm slip under my back, and another slip under my knees. I was scooped up and cradled, like a sleeping child protectively being carried to bed by a loving parent. I watched the rest of the scene unfold from above.

I stared down at a mess of vehicles. Even though my physical body was still in the car, I saw the accident as if through a hole in a layer of clouds, despite it being a sunny, cloudless day. While I peered through this opening with interest, I was aware I wasn't alone. I could feel the touch of one or two spiritual beings on my arms above the elbow.

The hole in the "clouds" was similar to when I was fifteen and found myself looking into another dimension, where I saw the sumo wrestler and my daughter who coaxed me back into my body. This time though, from my vantage point, I seemed to be looking from another dimension into this one, where I saw a car going in the opposite direction pull over on the other side of the road. I saw a person jump out and quickly run across the street to the accident.

I know people often stop to help at accidents, but why am I up here looking down on it? I thought. *Why am I seeing this from so high up in the air instead of from my physical body? What is this white, cloudy area I'm floating in? What is this gauzy hole I'm looking through?*

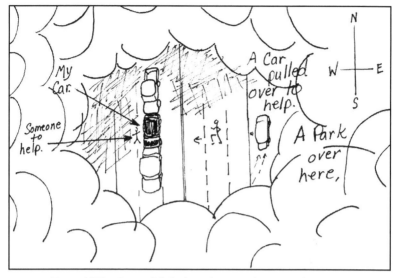

Figure 4 What I saw while looking down on the car accident scene.

Instantaneously, I snapped back into my physical body. My knees were bent and draped over the steering wheel with my legs hanging between the steering wheel and the dashboard. The column levers had been torn off by the force of my feet and legs being thrown into it. My upper body was still lying across the front seat, where I'd lain down, just as instructed by the voice I'd heard.

I could hear the whir of my car's engine. My glasses had been thrown from my face. I scrambled to sit up and reached for the ignition to turn the car off. I managed to accomplish this task, but I felt dizzy as I moved my body quickly back into what was left of the driver's seat.

I heard a man's voice ask if I was alright. I told him I was okay, but I'd lost my glasses, so he found them for me on the front passenger-side floor.

Suddenly, I felt a massive, gushing pressure within my body traveling to my head. I clutched my head between my hands. I felt like a human thermometer, as though a red line of pain and pressure was shooting up through my body and was about to explode out of the top of my head. I started moaning, saying that my head felt like it was going to burst.

I was told to lie down, by whom I don't know. When I tried to sit up, someone pushed me back into the seat. I heard a woman's voice saying with sureness, "The front seats are laid down, the driver must have been thrown into the back seat."

"Is that correct?" a man asked me, referring to the woman's statement, who I later found out was a nurse who stopped on her way to work.

"No," I replied. At the time, I didn't know that I'd actually been thrown into the back seat.

As you can imagine, my small hatchback had little chance against a massive pickup truck going forty miles per hour, and there wasn't much left of my car. It was only after I saw its mangled remains that I realized the front windshield was intact, but the rear hatchback window had been shattered and wasn't there anymore. In fact, I was lucky to have only been tossed into the back seat instead of having gone over the back seat into the trunk, where I would have been crushed by the oncoming truck.

The ambulance arrived. I remember only bits and pieces of the rescue, but I do recall arms reaching to put me on a board. I don't remember them removing me, strapping me onto the board, or loading me into the ambulance, but once I was in it, I felt intense pain. My shins were scraped badly when they were forced down between the dash and the steering wheel, so the pressure of the straps over the scrapes was agonizing. I whined and asked them to loosen the straps across my legs.

The paramedics relieved some of the tension up to a point, but told me they couldn't slacken them anymore. Suddenly, my body shook violently. The EMTs asked if I was cold, but I told them I wasn't. One of them said they'd better start an IV just in case. I don't know what "just in case" meant, but I assumed it had something to do with shock.

I must have seemed lucid to those around me, but my consciousness was mostly out of my body until later that day. I don't remember the ride to the hospital, the arrival at the hospital, or even seeing a doctor. I'm sure that if I had been physically unconscious, I would have been hooked up to all kinds of monitors, but I wasn't. To the medical personnel I must have *seemed* conscious, but in reality, no one was home in my body.

I came back to my body and experienced momentary lucidity at one point in the emergency room unit, when the curtains drew back and a police officer slipped in. He asked if I could talk with him for a moment. He inquired about the accident and wanted to see my driver's license.

I asked him for my purse, which was stowed away somewhere on the cart I'd been brought in on. He handed it to me, and I became confused because I couldn't find my license, even though I knew it was in my purse. The officer told me politely that it was okay and he would look it up. He asked if I'd run into the car in front of me. I explained to him that I'd come to a complete stop before the accident, and the analysis of the crash later confirmed this.

I was kept in the emergency room for observation, but later that afternoon when I was more coherent, the hospital staff said they would release me if I could find someone to pick me up. Few people had cell phones in those days; our telephone directories were our memories. The trauma had knocked me clueless, and I could only remember my friend Vicky's number—she was my mentor, my trainer at work, and my friend. Vicky was always there for me in times of need.

News of my accident traveled fast at work. The Area Manager's secretary called the hospital once she heard the news. The overwhelming concern and well-wishes conveyed by the secretary from the managers and staff where I worked, as well as Vicky over the phone while I lay in the hospital, proved once again how great that company and its people were.

When Vicky arrived later, she looked at me and tears came to her eyes. There were large splatters of blood on my shirt, but I don't know why—maybe from blood tests or something that I don't remember. The only abrasions I had were on my shins. Other than that, miraculously, I had no cuts or broken bones. Vicky took me to see my car, and the following photos are what I found. The man from the service department was amazed and relieved to see me alive. He thought that whoever had been in the car had been killed.

Figure 5 (above) The car from the side, windshield intact.

Figure 6 (above) The car from the rear-the window I saw shattering.

It is a genuine miracle that I survived the accident. In analyzing what happened, I can't ignore these facts.

God heard me when I thought, *Oh God, he's going to hit me!* I wholeheartedly believe my thought qualified as a call for His help. His answer was the voice that said, "Lie down across the seat and cover your face." God knows our thoughts and knows what we're going to say. This is referred to in Psalm 139:4-5 which I shared earlier, and God's presence in times of trouble is referred to in Psalm 46:1 as "our refuge and strength, always ready to help in times of trouble" (NLT).

I was saved by that voice and by an invisible figure with huge arms that picked me up. That invisible figure not only took my spiritual body up into the sky to look down on the scene, but it stayed with me. I knew it was there even though I couldn't see it. In Psalm 91:11, it says: "For he orders his angels to protect you wherever you go. They will hold you up with their hands to keep you from striking your foot on a stone" (NLT). The angels did this in my case—for sure.

Other spiritual helpers must have manipulated my physical body. I say this because my body had to have been placed just right to avoid any broken bones. It is a miracle that my legs and feet were not crushed, not to mention that after my body had been smashed around in the car, I ended up in the same position I'd started in, not realizing I'd even moved.

After I saw the mangled remains of my car, I realized the front windshield was intact, but the rear hatchback window had been shattered and wasn't there anymore. My car was totaled, and though I was very stiff and sore later and it took a long time for my body to heal from the muscle trauma, I had no broken bones, and was released from the hospital that same afternoon.

Was the nurse who arrived at the scene an angel sent by God, too? Had He choreographed the timing of events to coincide with her crossing my path at the time of the accident? Had He laid it on her heart to stop and help? Was it her car, heading in the opposite direction toward the hospital and other medical facilities, that I saw pull to the side of the road to assist? She most definitely is an earth angel if she wasn't actually a spiritual angel.

I am also overwhelmingly thankful that God orchestrated the invitation from my parents to spend time with my children. Their invitation protected them from being in the car with me that day.

When I woke up the next morning, I was a mess. Muscle trauma set in and my body stiffened—it got progressively worse over the weekend. I went to work on Monday with a cervical collar around my neck. My gait was stiff, and my steps were small and tight. My supervisor's office was located on the second floor, and there was no elevator. I could only climb the stairs a single footstep at a time, lifting the lower foot to the same tread as the first one, before continuing to the next when I needed to deliver papers to his office. I kept being told to go home, but it just wasn't like me to not work if I was capable. Besides, there was no one home to pass the time with if I did go home.

Even though nothing had been broken, I did sustain soft tissue damage and suffered from the difficulties associated with it. I saw an osteopath who helped to a certain extent, but eventually, I was referred to a spinal rehabilitation specialist.

My rehabilitation involved massage therapy several times a week to loosen my tight muscles and a regimen of exercises where the intensity gradually increased to strengthen the muscles. When we started out, it was so painful—the therapist's fingers felt like razor blades going up my body. The therapist thought I was overreacting, but it was excruciating.

The therapy continued for months, until I eventually graduated to a gym area where I could do further work on my muscles to get them back to where they should be. At the proper time, I was released to do the exercise on my own, which I continue to this day to keep the pain from returning.

My physical symptoms started to slowly progress into experiencing hundreds of what I can only call "electrical strikes" throughout my body. There was no set pattern; it felt like little lightning bolts striking the end of my toe, my thigh, my arm, my fingertips, and everywhere else. Each night I would grab the current romance novel I was reading and fall into bed still suffering from this electrical phenomenon. Reading romances was like a relaxing bubble bath that erased the stress of the day, but each night just as I tried to sleep, my body felt like it began to vibrate a little. It felt so strange it made sleep very difficult.

I saw my family doctor and asked him what was causing these unexplainable happenings. The doctor suggested I see a neurologist, so I scheduled an appointment with one that he recommended. I thought I should be prepared, so I found a simple outline of a woman's body and started marking the location of the electrical shocks as I got them. By this time, I was having well over a hundred per day.

I shared my concerns with the neurologist, and when he saw my drawing of the electrical shocks, he ordered an EEG. The day of the test, I went to the hospital and lay on a flat table. The technician turned flashing lights on and off. When a flashing light came on, my body vibrated violently like I was being bounced about on a speeding wagon careening over a bumpy road.

I didn't lose consciousness, and I knew exactly what was going on at all times. I was told to relax and not move. I did as I was instructed, and interestingly, it was not an unpleasant experience. I felt like I was looking down the length of my body through portholes.

The neurologist, after having reviewed the EEG results, told me these shocks were so-called myoclonic seizures. Myoclonus can develop after a head or spinal cord injury, in response to an infection, or for any of a number of reasons.[7] Once the doctor made the diagnosis, an anti-seizure medicine was prescribed to minimize the electrical shockwaves—eventually, they were hardly noticeable.

As I look back on the accident now and ponder everything I've been through since that fateful day, what amazes me the most is my absolute certainty that I was saved by divine intervention.

But I know one thing for sure about my accident: I was saved by an angelic being, possibly the angelic sumo wrestler that was my protector, or by the Divine himself. I called out to God, and He protected me. The Bible verse that holds immense significance for me now is Psalm 50:15, which states, "Call to

---

[7] "Myoclonus Information Page." NIH National Institute of Neurological Disorders and Stroke. Accessed November 14, 2017. http://www.ninds.nih.gov/Disorders/All-Disorders/Myoclonus-Information-Page

me in times of trouble. I will save you, and you will honor me"
(NCV).

I didn't know it at the time, but the way my life has unfolded
since that accident has proven to me that on that day, God was
going to make sure I would honor Him just as that Bible verse
says. God is a very creative thinker, but that doesn't surprise me:
He is the Creator of all.

4
CONSTRUCTION ZONE
The Ultimate Ambush Makeover

S IX YEARS AFTER MY car accident, my world fell apart. Some doctors say it was a delayed trauma from the crash, but no one was entirely sure. Could such a thing actually occur a full six years after a major shock? While that doesn't make sense, there really was no explanation for what caused my world to collapse.

Everything was going great. I'd fallen in love and married my long-time friend Gavin, who I had coffee with on the day of the car accident. By now, we had known each other for about six or seven years and had been married for several years. After we married, we had purchased a seventy-five acre ranch north of Denver and moved away from the city lights to the starlit nights of the country.

I'd worked for the same major corporation for many years, and had worked my way up the corporate ladder to Network Coordinator. My area of responsibility covered portions of seven states (approximately 250,000 square miles, or 350,000 square kilometers). For European readers, my area of responsibility would be roughly the size of three countries the size of Austria—or 1.6 the size of Germany. Suffice it to say, it was a large zone.

My duties included using company equipment and outside carriers to meet transportation needs for the company's product. This consisted of transferring product from the local plant to other company distribution centers and coordinating the transportation required for shifting product from plant to plant.

My job required a lot of outstanding analytical, interpersonal, and teamwork skills, but I didn't know that God gave me these skills to be useful in a far more significant way. How could I have known that my expertise and my passion for detail would also help me understand the spiritually transformative experiences I'd had (and the ones that were yet to come)? These skills have allowed me to understand the incredible depth of all my spiritual experiences.

Unbeknownst to me, it was when I was at the top of my game in my career when my "dark night of the soul" began. Overnight, I went from being a vibrant, intelligent person to being a catastrophe. The person I knew as Jan was being stripped and annihilated by an unseen force. None of what happened to me made any sense, because there was no precipitating event, no trigger—basically, no cause.

The seizures that had developed a month after the car accident had been kept well under control, but suddenly they got stronger. The electrical "snapping" sensations began to feel more like lightning bolts than little shocks. I felt like I was being bitten by a giant parakeet sized, hungry, energy-mosquito with a laser zapping sting. I would uncontrollably slap my body in the spots where the electrical power had swiftly snapped.

That was bad enough, but from one day to the next, my world fell apart. My ordinary reality was altered when my hands started shaking to the point that I couldn't write checks or even sign my name legibly. I stuttered and couldn't get words out of my mouth. I could see the picture of what I wanted to say inside of my head, but I couldn't recall the words to express it verbally.

This made managing coordinating efforts over the telephone impossible. I could no longer do math calculations (which had always been easy for me) and it physically hurt to think.

I fell into a depression that consumed me. My body felt as if it was a lead weight, and at times I felt like a shell with nothing inside. I knew that Jan was in there somewhere, but the energy of the person I knew as Jan was so microscopic, it felt like a tiny spark of light in a dark corner of the pit of my stomach.

However, as I write this, I've since had a third NDE, and I now see this is why God showed me during that NDE an image of this time frame with the "Construction Zone" sign. This is where God chose to overhaul my "software system." He'd saved me in the car accident, and now He wanted the honor that was due to Him.

I can only compare this experience to when a computer specialist wipes the hard drive of a computer clean and reinstalls better, more advanced program software. Unfortunately, with a human body, this reprogramming is a slow process, so the physical body can make the necessary adjustments to accommodate the new systems. We cannot immediately reboot ourselves successfully like a computer; rather, it takes time and repeated tunings to get the latest software up and running.

I now think of this change as the ultimate in "ambush makeovers," but God was not just making me over with fresh makeup, a new hairstyle and stylish clothing—He was remolding the core of my being. He was changing me from the inside out. The outdated software system of the person I knew as Jan was being updated with a more significant plan. God had more in store for me.

When I look back on this period of my life, I chuckle just a little because it reminds me of that famous comedy vaudeville show *The Three Stooges*—only I was all of the Stooges rolled into one. I was shaking and stuttering. I continually smacked myself to alleviate the pain of the electrical shocks that were striking my body. I walked around hitting various parts of my body, and yes, even slapping my own face. Moe, Larry, and Curly had nothing on me.

Slapping myself was embarrassing, especially when it happened during product planning meetings. On one occasion, after I'd done this several times, the Plant Manager, whom I was sitting next to, stopped the planning meeting, cocked his head so he could look at me, and with furrowed brows, asked if I was okay. What could I say? Oh my goodness! Can you imagine?

In my desperate quest for answers, I saw many doctors. I resorted to help from a psychiatrist, who also couldn't find a solution. I took a handful of medicines the doctors suggested, but nothing seemed to work. I wondered why nothing was getting me back to where I used to be.

I was referred to a Parkinson's specialist about the shaking and stuttering to see if it was Parkinson's disease. The doctor did tests, and after completing his evaluation, he said it was not Parkinson's, but psychosomatic. Interested to know more, I asked him what psychosomatic was, since I'd only heard the term but was not familiar with what it meant. Very kindly, he put his hand on my shoulder and compassionately told me that my subconscious mind was the culprit.

I was not insulted by the psychosomatic diagnosis; in fact, I was thankful that he was honest with me. That gave me a place to start working. I used one hand to stabilize the other to control my shaking. I used all my concentration to stare down and begin to control the wild, crazy motions.

The Parkinson's specialist gave my subconscious mind credit for causing these things to happen, but I'm not sure he knew the depth of precisely who the "subconscious" is. I didn't know it at the time, but God was going to reveal the answer to that question in the future. What we call the subconscious is actually our spiritual connection with Heaven, the Holy Spirit, which we also know as our soul. Little did my doctor know, that when he'd credited the subconscious mind with the power to make these types of things happen, he was really crediting God's own spirit.

5

MY PRAYER FOR HEALING AND JESUS'S CURATIVE TOUCH

FTER THE CAR ACCIDENT, I was drawn to church again for some reason. Maybe it was the memory of those huge arms that saved me and the knowledge there is a world around us we can't see that created this pull. I have to say, I'm not a religious person. This is due to the limitations many religions placed on God's abilities, so I'm more spiritual in nature.

I hadn't been to church since I was a child, so I was not familiar with the churches in the area. Fortunately, Gavin suggested and introduced me to a church he heard about. I enjoyed the messages because the talks were creatively related to today's society and gave a sense of hope and positivity. It was like listening to a motivational speaker rather than a dull sermon.

Once Gavin and I moved to the country years later, though, we didn't attend church. The type of churches we wanted to go to were now cities away and seemed just too far. But one day, Gavin received a call from his cousin Ted, who told him he was coming to Denver in September and hoped to see us. Gavin and Ted hadn't seen each other for untold years, so this was a surprise.

Ted was part of the Benny Hinn ministry group, and he generously offered to send us tickets to Benny's Miracle Crusade, since the group was meeting in Denver. Our ranch was a few miles outside of a small town in Colorado, not far from Denver. It was an easy drive for us when the Benny Hinn Ministries brought the Miracle Crusade to town.

I had not heard of Benny Hinn nor did I know what a miracle crusade was, but Gavin briefly told me that he was a pastor known to provide exceptional sermons. Did I want to go? I jumped at the chance. Mostly, I wanted to meet Ted, but I was also looking forward to hearing Benny's motivational sermon.

Interested to learn more about this man before attending the meeting, I read more about his life on his website, and later in his book *Good Morning Holy Spirit*. In Canada, Benny's life changed drastically when he had a transformative spiritual experience. The Holy Spirit appeared to him in a dream vision and that night his spiritual experience transformed his life. That was when the Holy Spirit became real to him. He started hearing a voice calling him to preach but he'd had a stuttering problem, which made him feel uncomfortable preaching. He didn't think it was possible, but as soon as he stood behind the podium, miraculously, his stuttering was cured.[8]

---

[8] Hinn, B. *Good Morning Holy Spirit*. Nashville: Thomas Nelson, Inc, 1997. E-book.

He is also well-known to be a channel of Jesus's healing powers. Sadly, with all the work I'd done to improve my health, I'd made only a little progress in my recovery from these debilitating electrical sensations. The electrical shocks persisted even though the medication calmed them; however, they continued to crop up when I was tired or run down. With everything I'd been through, I was experiencing a deep depressive state.

I thought about how Benny had had a stuttering problem in his earlier days, so I thought, *Why not me too? And while he's at it, could he heal the cognitive problems I'm being treated for as well?* What the doctors were doing wasn't working, so who better to turn to than Jesus? I asked Gavin if he'd support me by asking Ted to facilitate a healing for me from Benny, and Gavin agreed.

The date of meeting Gavin's cousin arrived, and we had the most perfect fall weather for the drive into Denver. I was looking forward to the opportunity to be in a church environment again, and Gavin was looking forward to seeing Ted. Our seats at the Pepsi Event Center were about ten rows back from the stage. I was so thrilled to be that close to the action! Upon our arrival, we had a pleasant walk in the sunshine from the far parking lot to the Pepsi Center looking forward to seeing Ted. We asked the usher to please let him know we'd arrived.

It wasn't long before Ted came out to greet us. We chatted, and Gavin asked Ted if he could speak to Benny about my healing. Ted said he wasn't sure he would even see Benny and couldn't promise anything, but that he'd try.

The sermon was gripping and moving, and the music and choir touched our souls with beautiful voices and heart-rending music.

We all asked for healing, as the crowd prayed and the choir sang. Benny and the choir led the crowd in worship. Some of the notable songs were "He's The Savior Of My Soul" initially written by Ada Blenkhorn but adapted in 1965 by Kathryn Kuhlman, and "He Touched Me" written by Bill Gaither. The energy in the complex from the dynamic sermon was electric with the crowd's desire to be healed from various ailments. After approximately an hour had gone by, Benny and the choir moved us into song again. Benny took his opportunity to slip off stage as the choir and the crowd continued to sing and pray.

I had never been a part of anything like this before, but as I was caught up in the music and words, I prayed to Jesus for a miracle healing. I prayed with my heart, my gut, and every fiber of my being. Suddenly, I felt an electric tingling in my head, like I'd been touched by a magic wand. The movie *Cinderella* came to mind, when her fairy godmother tapped Cinderella's head, and tiny, twinkling sparkles showered down over Cinderella. Suddenly, she transformed into the beautiful princess she'd truly always been. I got so dizzy I had to grab the chair in front of me. I felt sure that I'd been touched by the hand of Jesus.

Benny was taking a short break to ready himself for the miracle healings, so he was not on stage when I felt the touch of Jesus. Crusade staff asked that people who wanted to be healed to form a line up to the stage, and it grew fast. Gavin and I blended into the queue, but were too far back and never made it to the platform.

It didn't matter, because I knew something had happened, and it wasn't of great consequence to have had Benny as the vessel for healing. God had torn me down a few years previously, but through His sacred grace, Jesus had touched me and healed me Himself. This was just phase one of the healing I was to receive—He wasn't done with me yet.

On the drive home, I told Gavin what had happened during the prayers. I told Gavin that I felt sure that Jesus Himself touched me. I had no doubt it happened this way so I would know that it was by His own touch—not through Benny's—that I was healed.

I asked Gavin to give me some math calculations. Ever since my illness came on, I could no longer do multiplication tables, and any type of math was impossible. Gavin gave me a variety of multiplication problems: 3 x 3, 4 x 2, 5 x 5, etc. Miraculously, I knew the answers! When he asked me to multiply higher numbers like 6 x 7, however, it became difficult.

Before then, my mind was a fog—it hurt to think. Whenever I tried to analyze a problem or situation, my head physically hurt. I had to just learn to live in the moment. But in the car that day, I was excited. Gavin didn't know what to say, so I couldn't tell what he thought, but it didn't matter. As far as I was concerned, I had received healing.

6
THE FULFILLMENT OF MY PRAYER
Healing Phase Two

T HE UNUSUAL OCCURRENCES IN my life, like knowing things as a child I shouldn't have known, the Music Box Lady and Angelic Sumo man, and the divine intervention during the car accident, were so far apart that they remained separate, unexplainable events. Even though the door to my awareness had been cracked open after the Music Box Lady, I was able to shelve it.

However, after the divine intervention, I could no longer ignore that there was something out there I couldn't see and it was pulling me back to the love God was eager to share. Now, after the fairy godmother-like touch of Jesus, my senses were on high alert to all the unusual occurrences around me.

The healing I received that night of the Miracle Crusade was not a total body healing, but it was the healing I needed at the time. The treatment Jesus provided made it easier for me to think without pain. After my divine makeover, I learned to go with the flow and to live in the moment, in order to avoid the physical discomfort of intellectual reasoning. This forced me to seek the answers I needed within my heart instead of my questioning mind. Was this God's way of setting the stage for His next miracle?

As I relived the songs and prayers from the day of the Miracle Crusade, I was drawn back in time to those moments. I experienced the depth of emotion I'd felt in my soul as I prayed to Jesus for healing. I remembered the song called "He's the Savior of My Soul" that the audience sang in praise and worship. Ms. Kuhlman's lyrics guided us to acknowledge that Jesus was the savior of the soul, just as the title of the song suggests. At the time, I didn't know that there would be even more significance in this song later in my life.

As we sang "He's the Savior of My Soul," Benny Hinn had encouraged us to lift our hands to Heaven and speak the name of Jesus, so we sang with our hands outstretched upward, calling the name of Jesus. The energy was electrified, and the feeling of the crowd was profound and moving; the whole audience was caught up in devotional praise.

Then, we transitioned into the song "He Touched Me" by Bill Gaither. Bill Gaither's amazing song describes the power of God's touch and how it could transform a life.

Another hymn we used in our prayers were the lyrics to "Breathe Upon Me Breath of God" by Benny Hinn. This song reminded me of the breath of God that is said to have brought life to mankind.

Also within the mix of hymns was "Jesus, You're All I Need" by Darlene Zschech, which also was significant to the prayer God was going to answer.

It wasn't until, over ten years later, when I watched a video of the Benny Hinn event that I remembered the songs and lyrics in detail, which I'd included in my prayers that night. I realized that not only had my prayers been answered precisely as I requested, but the lyrics of the songs and hymns were vital to the healing I received a few years later when God, Jesus, and the Holy Spirit completed the answer to my prayer.

I realized as I viewed the video that Jesus had given me part of the physical healing I wanted when I went to the Miracle Crusade; nevertheless, He knew that was not the most essential healing I needed. Nor was it what I was actually praying for while we worshiped using the words to these songs. The words to the songs called for a healing of the soul, not physical healing. The actual fulfillment of my healing prayers was to be delivered during my third NDE when I receive the spiritual healing I was really praying for.

ABOUT TWO AND A half years after the Miracle Crusade, I had my third near-death experience at our ranch near Denver, Colorado. To reach our house, visitors had to drive up a one-quarter-mile gravel driveway. Just north of the house, they passed a grove of trees that protected our home, barns, corrals, and outbuildings from the brisk north winds and the dust raised by cars driving up the country road.

On our ranch, we had horses, a dog, and thirteen cats. Cats are a rancher's best friend, since they help keep rodents away. Our animals were like family members, and each had their own personality. Every morning Gavin and I, with our Australian Shepherd, Patch, would jump out of bed as the sun was rising (sometimes before) to feed the horses. If the sun was up, we freed the cats from their safe sanctuaries, and if not, the person who left for work last would open the doors so the cats could start their day, too.

Every evening after work, we fed the horses and ensured that all the animals had plenty of water. The cats returned to the yard after their excursions in the fields, which must have felt like a jungle to them. They relaxed, stretched, and looked for a little love from us when we finished our chores—which, most of the time, we were happy to provide.

Before sunset, Patch would go and sit by the door of a barn. That was the signal to the cats that it was time for them to take shelter for the evening. Before we'd implemented this proce-dure, I had to catch—even lure—all of our "fur balls" and carry them into the buildings. Eventually, they learned that they had to be indoors for their own protection—packs of coyotes roamed the region and cats are a yummy coyote treat.

So, the cats cooperated, bedtime worked well, and all the animals were secure. Each cat chose to sleep in a space in one of the two barns or in one of several outbuildings. It was remarkable how they divided themselves up—the same cats always went into the same buildings, and each had a space they called their own.

The coyotes wouldn't bother larger animals, but they wreaked havoc with the smaller ones in and around the ranch.

Every night, we heard them howl, letting one another know where they were. They yelped with excitement whenever they caught their prey—a poor, unsuspecting rabbit, or a gopher in the wrong place at the wrong time. Any small animal was a perfect dinner for them, including Patch.

At night, when I took Patch out to relieve himself, I carried a large flashlight—more like a searchlight, really—so I could see the surrounding yard, the horse run, and into the grove of trees. Every dark spot was a potential hideout for an annoying coyote. Since we often worked after dark completing our ranch-related chores, we put floodlights around the house and barns to discourage the coyotes. That made it less frightening to be outside at night, and we didn't have to be so vigilant about safety.

As you can imagine, there was a lot to do on the ranch. It was a never-ending cycle of work, but we enjoyed ranch life immensely—especially the expansive view of the entire front range. We could see the snow on Pikes Peak, over three hours south of us. The night sky was gorgeous, with millions of stars that we couldn't see in the city, all twinkling above us on clear evenings.

During the spring and summer, I loved to decorate the area around the house with large, decorative pots, with flowers that cascaded over the sides. They were placed in strategic locations at various points along the front and sides of the house to welcome visitors to our home.

We had lived at the ranch for many years, but at one point, I developed what appeared to be a seasonal allergy. To alleviate the discomfort of my stuffy nose and congestion, I took an over-the-counter decongestant at night. As the seasons changed, I expected the symptoms to go away, but they didn't. I didn't realize at the time that my symptoms bothering me came from inside the house, not outside.

One night, after taking a decongestant, I climbed into bed and stacked three pillows on top of each other, so my body was at a forty-five-degree angle when I lay down—this position helped me breathe better. I wasn't aware at the time that fragrances were the trigger for my congestion, and I had a scented plug-in next to the bed. I also cleaned everything with scented products and used scented shampoos, soaps, lotions, and detergents. On this particular night, my body finally decided it had had enough of these scented products.

I fell asleep with Gavin lying next to me. During the night, I felt a tightening in my chest. The allergy had closed off my airway. My chest felt like it was being squeezed in a vice. I struggled to sit up, hoping to catch my breath, but I didn't have the strength. I reached for Gavin with my left hand to let him know I was in trouble, but my hand never made contact with his body. It seemed to just go through him.

He didn't respond, so I yelled, "Help me, Gavin! Help me!" But still, Gavin slept.

Suddenly, I was floating at ceiling level, looking down at my body and I thought, *Hey, that's me down there!* Even though we had turned the light off when we went to bed, the room glowed softly. Suddenly, I realized I didn't feel the pain in my chest anymore. I had a strong feeling that I can only describe as having been "set free from captivity."

I felt infinite! I felt ecstatic and unburdened! In my very essence, I felt surrounded with—no, infused with—the most incredible sense of peace and an unbounded, rapturous love. I realized I was experiencing the scene from the point of view of my spirit-body, that "I" was hovering over my physical form. Additionally, I felt a connection to high universal knowledge. How can anyone adequately express these deeply spiritual sensations?

When I was in my body, I felt like the compressed contents of a balloon that had been blown to capacity with helium. Now, the balloon was taut with pressure, unable to expand any further; but at that moment, it was as if that helium balloon suddenly exploded and released me into the atmosphere. Or like a woman wearing a corset so tightly tied that she can barely breathe or move, but suddenly, the laces break open, releasing the woman from bondage. Can you imagine that sense of freedom? That's how it felt, but more intense, like I could finally draw in a giant breath of relief. After that refreshing breath, I felt like I was floating in a vastness of the most ineffable, profound peace and a love that I've never imagined possible.

Many years after this NDE, I had LASIK eye surgery to improve my vision, but as I noted earlier, when this NDE occurred, my eyesight was poor. I wore contact lenses during the day and always kept my glasses next to my nightstand. But, in spirit form, my sight was perfect. It was fascinating to me that I was floating, peaceful and free, near the ceiling but also acutely aware of my surroundings.

When I looked upward toward heaven, the ceiling had suddenly vanished. All I could see was blackness; nonetheless, this seemed reasonable. It was the middle of the night, after all. I thought it was odd, though, that I didn't see the moon or any stars. When I glanced around the room below me, everything was slightly aglow. *Where is the light coming from?* I wondered. I wasn't afraid—I felt as though I was flowing in perfect harmony with All That Is. I knew that everything was normal because I'd been here before.

I floated above the ceiling, as if the roof had melted away, so I had an unobstructed view of the room below. I was drifting slightly to the right, above my body. Suddenly, I noticed a pin of light off to the right side of my body. In spiritual form, I could see in all directions at the same time. The light traveled toward me and grew as it approached. Again, I wasn't afraid.

Since I wasn't concerned about the light and I could see in all directions at the same time, I chose to concentrate on my physical body. I felt similar to a doctor standing on the right-hand side of her patient's bed, but I was watching from a much higher viewpoint—ceiling height.

My body lay in the same position I'd been in when I had stretched out to sleep, propped up on the pillows, with both hands clasped over my tummy. Suddenly, I realized that my left hand hadn't actually reached for Gavin as I'd thought it had—I'd been reaching with my "spirit arms," not my physical ones. That's why I couldn't feel Gavin's body, and why he hadn't responded when I had yelled.

My curiosity was piqued. I wanted to study the body of that person I knew was me—and suddenly, I zoomed down, looking at my body from all different directions. A part of me realized I must be dead, but that didn't bother me—I was detached from my body both physically and emotionally.

Mindful of all that was going on, I realized that I felt physically detached because I was no longer in that cumbersome mode of transportation that restricted me. I felt emotionally detached because that body wasn't the "real me," and I didn't care to go back into it, thank you very much—so I returned to the ceiling. I was aware that my spiritual arms were elongated and floated out to my sides. I knew that my spirit body could stretch out as far as it needed to, to release itself from the physical body, and that it could change form as it desired.

As I floated toward the ceiling again, I saw a silver cord that looked like an umbilical cord. It moved gently across my field of vision from left to right. It looked like a small hose floating out of the hand of an astronaut fixing the outer capsule of a space station, drifting, in zero-gravity, in mid-space.

I saw my entire house as if there was no roof. Oddly, as I moved higher into the atmosphere, I observed the layout of the inside, as well as the outside of the house and all its rooms, but I kept my focus mostly on the bedroom, where the action was. I noticed movement and saw something starting to lift out of my physical body. It rose up, out of my feet, my shins, my thighs, and my hips.

I realized that the spiritual energy that remained in my body was escaping and that I, the viewer, was the "upper half" of that same spirit body. I was connected to that lower, ethereal body but I was stretched out, watching the rest of my astral body detach from its earthly shell. While I witnessed all of this spirit-activity,

I was ultra-aware of my identity as "Jan," because I continued to retain all her thoughts and memories. I was, I realized, an energetic body of consciousness that had been inhabiting this human being known as "Jan."

I call this form of pure energy my spirit, my soul, or my consciousness because, to me, they all refer to the same thing. The idea that human consciousness needs a brain to exist is entirely wrong. I know this because my mindful sense of "oneness with all things" occurred in all three of my near-death experiences. All of my NDEs have proven to me that, honestly, we never die. Our soul retains our life lessons and memories as we travel from this material world to the eternal continuum of eternity.

In movies dealing thematically with death, filmmakers often depict characters as seeing spirits rising out of their bodies that mirror the shape and likeness of their physical bodies, only misty, filmy, or transparent. This is not *initially* what happened in my experience. When my spirit was fully released from the lower half of my body, it was a blue, translucent, shimmering essence that rose into the air like lava in a lava lamp. The blue was the luminous shade of an exquisite, cloudless sky and somehow I knew this was my own personal portion of the Holy Spirit.

I was still floating far above my body, looking down, taking in the whole scene, ultra-aware of all the minute details around, above, behind, and below me. My attention reverted to the pinpoint of light that had been in the distance, which was now getting closer. It approached in a slight S-shaped curve, moving faster and faster. Imagine an airplane in flight—from a distance, a plane seems to be moving slowly, but it zips by you in a flash when it gets closer. This pin of light didn't pass by me, however; instead, it flew into the room and stopped. Then, it grew from a tiny pinpoint of light into a brilliant, luminescent being.

The figure had long hair, and the light emanating from it was so spectacular and bright I couldn't see its facial features. I thought initially that it was female because of the hair length, since most men I know have short hair. But this radiant light-being had the hips and stature of a male. It occurred to me that maybe it was a woman with a man's physique, but as it turned out, I was wrong.

The magnificent light surrounding this holy being was so bright that if you saw it with your earth-vision, you would need to shield your eyes. The light rays emanated from all around the being and from its heart; in fact, its entire essence was glowing. I realized, however, that part of the luminosity which made it impossible to discern its features was coming from me—I too was infused and glowing with light.

The light-being's chestnut-colored hair hung down onto its shoulders and it knew me. It knew everything about me—my successes and my failures—and in spite of everything, it didn't judge me. It only radiated divine love and I knew it was happy to see me. Its beauty was so celestial, marvelous, and awe-inspiring that I choked up with admiration and couldn't speak.

The bright light radiating through the locks caught their chestnut tones clearly. A delicate breeze seemed to lift strands of its hair and blow them lightly across its face. It wore a floor-length white gown, secured at the waist with a light brown, braided rope, the excess dangling gently down its front. As the light-being stood with its arms open wide in a welcoming gesture, its sleeves draped loosely from its wrists.

As I beheld this heavenly figure, I seemed to be facing it. I saw, off to the left, that another pin of light had appeared. It too was moving toward me in a slight S-shaped fashion, getting larger as it approached.

By this time, my blue, sky-colored spirit body had completely detached from my physical body, and I could feel my essence morphing into one unit, which felt to me like an orb. My vision became panoramic as the transformation took place. At first, it was twisted, as though I were looking out of a fishbowl, but when the fishbowl effect quickly melted away, my vision was superb.

I knew that my soul could take as many forms as it needed to or wanted to, but once the blue essence had separated entirely from my physical body I became the "orb-like being"—I could sense but could not see. I could not see myself in this state of being because I couldn't reach my hands out or view myself as I used to. I had the distinct sensation that I was this tiny orb, and that the light-being I was hovering in front of was seven-feet tall.

I want to explain what being drawn into this orb-like entity felt like, but there are few human words that can accurately describe these other-worldly sensations. It felt as though my energetic body enjoyed this breath of relief, but now it gathered itself together again. I could feel it pulling upward and inward combining once again into a single unit of energy that was me. Once the transformation was complete, I was a bubbly orb of light.

Once I changed to a spherical shape, I felt like I was resting not in an inner tube, but in one of those wands that children use to blow soapy bubbles with. I was being held in a shape like that—a bubble-blowing wand made of pure love.

Feeling like I was a bubble sitting in a wand is significant because it connects the experience to the words I used in my prayer of healing during the Miracle Crusade. When I sang the hymn "Breathe Upon Me Breath of God," I always heard that it was the breath of God that creates all things—and amazingly, it's written in the Bible that it was Jesus's breath that conveyed the Holy Spirit to his disciples after he rose from the dead.

The conveyance of the Holy Spirit through Jesus's breath is referred to in John 20:21-22: "As he spoke, he held out his hands for them to see, and he showed them his side. They were filled with joy when they saw their LORD! He spoke to them again and said, 'Peace be with you. As the Father has sent me, so I send you.' Then he breathed on them and said to them, 'Receive the Holy Spirit'" (NLT).

I genuinely believe that giving me this bubble sensation was God's clever way of making me aware that He orchestrated this NDE. He designed my NDE to match what I prayed for that night in Denver at the Pepsi Event Center.

The second pin of light kept coming through the darkness, approaching in the distance behind the light-being. I looked back at the light-being, and though I couldn't see his face, I knew he was smiling. He held his right hand toward me, palm-up, in a gesture that conveyed, *Come, take my hand, I'll take you home.*

By then, the pin of light had grown to become a magnificent and brilliant light of the purest love that can't be

Figure 7 My third NDE with the living light of God on left and Jesus on right.

found here in this mortal world. The light was alive and seemed like a tunnel. Clouds bubbled up around the radiant light in the shape of a cornucopia, which appeared to be sucking me gently into it. I thought then that the breeze that was blowing the light-being's hair was emanating from this cloud-tunnel, and that self-same breeze was drawing me inward with a gentle suction.

I knew I was supposed to go to the light, and as I focused on the light radiating from the tunnel, I knew it was the Living Light of God in all his essence. Every sense of imperfection I had during the life as Jan was erased in its presence and replaced with the knowledge that I was a spirit of flawless perfection. I didn't study the cornucopia shape intricately, but it was the bubbling effect of the clouds around it that gave it that hollow, horn-shaped-cloud appearance. Again, it was a delightful reminder to realize that in Revelation 1:7 it says, "Look! He comes with the clouds . . ." (NLT).

I don't know if the light-being and I were being drawn toward the light or if the light had come through the darkness. But it was close to us, on the light-being's right-hand side. It shone brilliantly, and I felt unimaginable colorful rays radiating from it, even though the light looked, for the most part, white.

I knew the colors were there. I'd become one with that light and with the colors, as if they were in everything and were everywhere. As I drifted even closer to the light, I felt the arms of God reach out to embrace me with healing, peace, and love. The infusion of extraordinary, higher knowledge that had started the moment I was released from my body intensified and was accompanied by the flashing by of film strips. As I viewed the images, God communicated a message that seemed to come from everywhere. His voice was gentle and it seemed like a whisper as He conveyed His important message: "*These moments matter. Understand them.*"

These moments are what this book is based on. Everything in and of this world of ours (and more) now made perfect sense. I saw and still see "the bigger picture." God gave me the gift of inner knowledge. Inner knowledge is the ability to spiritually understand the guidance of the soul and to understand God's will.

The Creator's subtle voice communicated that these moments were important and were designed for a purpose. I felt that once I'd entered the Light, I would know even more about pure love and absolute knowledge, but what I felt at that moment was already indescribable. I felt at home, safe, protected, and loved like I'd never felt before. I didn't want to go back--I wanted to understand the moments when I entered heaven instead of understanding the moments while staying in the mortal world. There wouldn't be a single soul that would ever want to leave the embrace of this Light and the feeling of peace and contentment It gave. The unbounded love that God has for each of us is so extraordinary no words can adequately convey the strength and power it holds and He is waiting for us to accept it.

I looked at the light-being, and in the most loving, telepathic voice, it said, "Jan, it's time to come home."

I hesitated. I was concerned about how my daughter Gina would take my death. She was more dependent on me than my sons. It answered my thought instantly: "She'll be okay."

Knowing that Gina would be alright, I decided to join the Light and go back to heaven. But God or Jesus—I'm not sure who—wanted to show me the future and what would happen if I did. Suddenly, my spherical body transformed into an energetic human form and I felt a gentle pressure on my elbows as I was whisked high into the sky with at least two other spiritual beings who didn't interfere, but stayed behind me. Even though I didn't turn to look upon their heavenliness, I could see their intense white and golden glow radiating around me. I don't know who the other beings were, but I imagine they were my guides or angels.

From several hundred feet in the air, I could still see my bedroom, but it was much smaller. I could see our house inside and outside, our yard, our neighbors' houses in the distance, and the surrounding land in all directions. As I floated there with the other beings, my attention was drawn to a vehicle far off in the distance, racing up the road toward our ranch. I could hear its tires on the gravel road and see its lights.

Strangely, it was as though my ears were right next to its tires. I heard the crunching of the tires as they rolled over the gravel, even though from my perspective, the vehicle was tiny. Its headlights were on, approaching in the darkness from far away. I also felt the bumps in the road as if I were riding along in the vehicle. This proves to me that our spiritual body (the Holy Spirit) can be in many places at the same time, just like God can.

As the vehicle turned into our quarter-mile-long driveway, I saw it was an ambulance. There was one deeply rutted area on our road where drivers had to be careful, and I saw the vehicle lurch as it hit that section. Even though I was high in the air observing this, I heard and felt the sounds and motions of the ambulance like I was inside the vehicle. I was also aware of myself and my husband in the bedroom below until he moved and was now waiting in the living room for help to arrive. From my vantage point high in the air, I had all perspectives.

The ambulance pulled up to the door at the side of the house that opened on to the porch, the mudroom, and the kitchen. The emergency personnel rushed in, and behind them, rescuers who arrived in a fire engine. The EMTs that could fit into our small bedroom did just that—I could see from my vantage point that there were also two people in the living room conversing and two more in the kitchen.

I was so high in the air I could only see where they were and that they were bent over my body, but I couldn't see what they were doing. I only know their movements and activity didn't seem overly swift. Maybe this was because we lived so far away from quick emergency help and there was no doubt I was dead before they even got there. I don't know, but I knew I was being shown I was going to die anyway. My death was what Heaven wanted me to see.

All of a sudden, I was down before the Living Light of God again. The immensity of God was in everything around me, as if I were a fish swimming in an ocean, not realizing that God was the water itself. God had come forth from the darkness, a bright tunnel of living light, filled with unconditional love and peace for me and all of humanity. I was on the precipice of entering this glorious light—I couldn't have gotten any closer without being inside of it. But first, Heaven wanted me to know something else.

God or Jesus—again, I don't know who—showed me a holographic image of my son, Curt, as a clean-cut, handsome young man. I knew he was going to need me in the future. If I didn't stay, Curt's future would be altered. This must have already been written, and I must have been aware, somehow, that his sacred journey was going to unfold in that way. I knew that it was imperative for me to help Curt.

After I saw Curt, I told the Light-Being telepathically, "I'm not ready to go yet." I knew He smiled, and immediately I was again that sky-blue spirit body. Instantly, I sat down in Jan's physical body as it lay on the bed. I watched my spirit legs in front of me settle into Jan's legs and feet, but not entirely. Then I—as my spirit body—held on to my knees and rocked back and forth in Jan's body, picking up momentum until I could help Jan sit up to catch a breath. She gasped for air and as she did, I—Jan's spirit body—settled into her.

As I was getting back into my body, I heard a message from Heaven. I already knew it from having been melded with God's consciousness, but Heaven wanted me to remember, so the words echoed over and over again. This divine message was imbued in my very core, and I'll remember it forever. The echoing message was not only for me—it is for everyone. This beautiful voice kept repeating:

Love is the only thing that matters.

I came back into my body with memories of specific past events in my life which I've already described. Yet there were other moments that still remained unidentifiable, but God wanted me to know these occasions in time were important.

I HAVE SINCE FOUND out that life reviews are typical for those who have had NDEs. Frequently, they are shown a holographic video of their life thus far, and they can evaluate their words and deeds from their own perspective, as well as from the viewpoint of others they interface with. They feel others' emotions and see the ripple effect of their human interactions. The visions I received may have been a life review, because I have had memories where I could have improved myself. However, some of the visions I recognized but hadn't immediately understood their meaning as God wanted me too, and others I didn't recognize because they hadn't happened yet. For instance, some visions that I hadn't understood yet contained elements like oil drilling equipment; a quaint little building with a Namaste sign; a group of indistinct men in white robes milling around in a haze of whiteness; my parent's home with me standing in the living room, where I don't ordinarily stand; my brother Doug; and

I could go on. I do know; however, I was being shown these events because He wanted me to know these were special destination points in my life that were important.

I was also very distressed about the vision of Curt and the meaning of the other visions I was shown. I had made a choice to stay to help my son, but didn't know what was going to occur. I sat up the rest of the night and cried. I knew something had happened, but I didn't know what. I did know that I wasn't ready to die, and now I had to live wondering when the other shoe was going to drop concerning Curt.

I started sleeping on the couch, halfway sitting up so I could breathe better. At the time, I didn't realize I slept better there because I wasn't next to a scented plugin. I bought face masks to filter the air. I felt silly wearing a mask around the house, and I'm sure everyone who came over thought I was crazy, but I knew something in the air had caused my allergic reaction. This was the only way I could think of to protect myself.

I scheduled an appointment with an allergist. My son Curt had allergies, and he was allergic to cats, so I thought perhaps I'd developed a cat allergy, too. I couldn't get into the allergist's office for quite some time.

At that time, it was fall and it was chilly outside. One of our cats had delivered a litter of kittens, and we built a protective cage for her and her offspring out on the heated porch. We thought this would keep the kittens safe and warm while they grew, and it also prevented their mother, Stripes, from hiding them somewhere among all the shelving and boxes the basement had to offer—like mother cats do. Eventually, Stripes was eager to join the other adult cats outside investigating the fields, but her kittens were still too vulnerable, so they stayed inside.

The kittens were darling, and we often brought them from the mudroom into the private house to cuddle them. We decided we'd keep them inside over the winter and move them outside come springtime. But when I had my NDE and I thought the cats might have precipitated my allergy, I wanted to fix up another shed with places for them to sleep, keep warm, and be protected from the coyotes.

Gavin, however, thought it was best to wait until spring—so, the cats moved inside the house, and I ended up sleeping in the office/library, which was a separate room attached to the house, only accessible through the mudroom where shoes are kept. This was a room where the cats weren't allowed into. I breathed better there, and I thought it was because it was a cat-free zone.

In fact, as I learned later, it was because there were no scented plugins in the office.

I found out later from the allergist that I'd developed a sensitivity to some man-made chemicals, including certain perfumes and scented products. I quite often refer to this sensitivity as an allergy because it's easier for people to understand its severity. The doctor prescribed inhalers to get me through the worst episodes and told me to systematically eliminate products around the house until I found out what I was reacting to.

Through trial and elimination, I found out that the air fresheners that gave the house a pleasing holiday season scent, especially the apple-pies-fresh-from-the-oven fragrance, were one of the leading culprits. I had one plugged into the electrical socket right next to my side of the bed! I changed every scented product in the house, including dryer sheets, fabric softener, laundry soap, dish soap, deodorant, and hair products.

After the third NDE, more intense sensitivities and unusual occurrences happened. I also noticed I was suddenly more aware of how people felt emotionally. Sometimes this was pleasurable because I could feel the loving nature of the person. I could also sense the difficulties they had in life, although I didn't at the time know exactly what those difficulties were. Other times I knew the other person's real feelings even though they were outwardly trying to mask the thoughts they were having.

Similarly, another way the energetic aftereffect manifested was I became hypersensitive. I could feel the energy of people and places acutely. After my NDE, Gavin and I visited a nearby store that sold groceries, clothing, and household supplies. I'd been in the store often and had never felt any ill effects, but after my NDE, the energy swirling around overwhelmed me.

There were too many people, too much color, too much sound, and too much movement—it all made me dizzy, nauseous, and faint. This sensitivity also caused negative words and actions to hit my psyche like an energetic fist to the abdomen. I seemed to be sensing their thoughts, and their energy that swirled around them. All of this was coming at me like it was flowing down a fast river, careening over a high waterfall, and I was standing at the bottom of the crashing water. I was pelted with all this information that felt like debris and I didn't want to be in the flow that was hitting me. All of this information was too fast. I didn't know where it was coming from, or why it was happening. Often, I needed to ask Gavin to finish the shopping while I waited in the car. I didn't know it at that time, but I was having an energy-overload anxiety attack. This symptom eased over the years, but I also learned to control where I went, and who I was with, to minimize the effects.

Sadly, these things started occurring many years before I learned about NDEs and aftereffect phenomena, so this was a confusing part of my life. It's no wonder so many adult NDErs' marriages fall apart with all of this strangeness going on. Poor Gavin had to go through these things, too.

Most mornings and afternoons after chores were done, a large number of local farmers and ranchers would gather for breakfast or in the afternoon for coffee and dessert. One day I unquestionably heard someone behind me call my name, but once I turned to see who was trying to get my attention, no one was there. This happened several times and I could sense the emotions of confusion the others at the table were feeling about my actions, so I chose to ignore the calls.

I was also now hyper-aware of energy disturbances around me that indicated there was something there I couldn't see. One evening in the library, I sat on the floor going through some papers. Our dog Patch was with me. I could feel the presence of something I couldn't see, and I was not the only one—Patch could sense it, too. He sat beside me, looking at the very same place I did.

Once I moved back into the house, when Gavin and I were in bed at night, I felt light impressions of something coming on to the bed. It felt like the footsteps of an invisible cat that was coming up to snuggle. We had a few furry fuzzballs that fell victim to feline leukemia or the hazards of the rattlesnakes or coyotes that lived in the area. Was this one of them coming to snuggle? When I moved to look, the movement would stop.

This reminds me of a different occasion, when I was sitting cross-legged on the library floor sifting through papers. Suddenly, my eyesight was drawn toward the open French door of the library. I was astounded when I looked out into the heated porch area and saw a cat who had seemingly come from the basement stairs. Patch was with me at the time and I noticed with my peripheral vision that he could see it too. However, the odd thing about this cat was that it was translucent. It walked in front of the clothes washer, dryer, and country sink continuing its casual walk in our direction, then it lifted its eyes and saw us too. We locked eyes and watched each other until it started turning to the right around the water heater. Then its head rotated back to where it was headed and disappeared, walking through the solid back door that was closed. Could this have been another spirit cat that had met its fate here? Amazingly the translucent cat looked exactly like Fraidy, one of our cats in the barn. Fraidy was afraid of everything except me. Could it have been her spirit who was investigating the house while its body slept in the barn?

I AM OFTEN ASKED, "How long were you dead, Janet?"

My answer is always, "I have no idea," because the NDE occurred in the middle of the night and Gavin slept through most of it. As I noted in the story of my NDE at fifteen, in the Bible, it says that a day is like a thousand years, and a thousand years is like a day. Time on the other side does not exist as it does here.

I know now that the chemical allergy I developed was Heaven-sent since it sparked my NDE. It was the catalyst that changed my life for the better in every way. After I came to this realization, I saw Jesus watching me with His arms crossed, nodding His head in acknowledgment.

After the NDE, I moved on with my life, and over time, the fragrance sensitivity seemed to miraculously subside, but I remain cautious about what I choose to wear. It's important to note this move was setting the conditions for me to help my son, Curt, in the way he needed.

This fantastic NDE proves to me that God controls our health in many ways. He can cause illness or allergy (sometimes as a catalyst for an NDE), or to motivate us to make a change in our lives to help someone. He can touch us with his finger and heal our bodies, and better yet, He can heal our souls.

Now that I've seen my soul and the silver cord that binds each of us to Heaven, I know that our souls are our personal share of God's Holy Spirit. God gives our bodies a soul as a guide to assist us in making the best choices to navigate our lives while we are living here. Our soul, also, is the energy that fuels our body forward, and once that energy returns to heaven, the body ceases to function. We can say that we are all divine because we house a part of God's Holy Spirit inside of us and without the Spirit, the body wouldn't live. Our partnership is essential to both the body and the soul.

I find it fascinating that in the Bible, we find a "rainbow of colors" mentioned, which was very similar to what I experienced that night: "The one sitting on the throne was as brilliant as gemstones – jasper and carnelian. And the glow of an emerald circled his throne like a rainbow" (Rev. 4:3 NLT).

The Bible refers to this same type of "silver cord" in Ecclesiastes 12:6-7: "Yes, remember your Creator now while you are young, before the silver cord of life snaps…and the spirit will return to God who gave it" (NLT). While there is some controversy concerning the author and the meaning of the Book of Ecclesiastes, from my viewpoint, I find divine inspiration in this book—not to mention that I actually saw the cord that is described there.

On several occasions, I have seen round orb shapes in photographs. They fascinate me. I reflected on the orb experience I'd had—floating in front of the light being who proved to be Jesus—and I analyzed it in hindsight. Had I been the same kind of pin-type light that had zoomed into the room and changed into Jesus?

As I pondered this, I became sure that I had indeed been small that night of the NDE. Remember how, when I was fifteen, I saw the sumo wrestler and music box lady convert themselves into balls of light when they left my room? It seems to me that this tiny spark—or ball of light—is a spirit form's mode of transportation. They morph, as it were, into a sphere of light we call an "orb."

I knew that everything that was happening at that moment was from God. And even though I didn't know for sure at the time that the light-being was Jesus, Jesus revealed that truth to me later—and later, I will share that revelatory moment with you. But I see now that this whole NDE experience matches perfectly what Jesus tells us in John 14:3-4: "When everything is ready, I will come and get you so that you will always be with me where I am. And you know where I am going and how to get there" (NLT). I had died, and Jesus had come for me, to show me the way home!

Now, after understanding the visionary moments I was shown during the third NDE, I realized from the moment I was saved during the car accident, all trivial traces of doubt about the existence of an invisible world had vanished from my mind. But now I see the collision was another step God had taken to cracking open the door of my awareness even more to His presence. At the time I was not aware of its spiritual significance nor had I heard of an NDE yet, so I turned to medical professionals for answers.

Much later in life, I read more about Benny Hinn's life in his book, *Good Morning Holy Spirit* and I found it very interesting that Benny's life changed drastically when he had the transformative spiritual experience (STE). This reminded me of how my life and the lives of others who have experienced NDEs or STEs were changed, too. The Holy Spirit appeared to him in a dream vision and seemingly scooped him up to heaven[9]. That night, his spiritual experience transformed his life and the Holy Spirit became

---

[9] Hinn, B. *Good Morning Holy Spirit*. Nashville: Thomas Nelson, Inc, 1997. E-book.

real to him, just like it did to me too. I also find it interesting that, similar to Benny, many experiencers receive a special mission to carry out. And like Benny, some are now known to be a channel for Jesus' healing touch too.

There was much significance in the songs we prayed to the night of the Miracle Crusade because on this night of my most significant NDE, he touched me and changed my life just like the song "He Touched Me" depicted. Not only did God come during my NDE, but Jesus and the Holy Spirit, too. All the super powers that I called to while singing the songs that night came to answer my request. Now I will never let them go. They are indeed all I need, just like the lyrics of the songs we sang that night in Denver at the Pepsi Center.

Often, I look at a clear blue sky and remember that it is the same color as my soul. I wonder if the very atmosphere is God's Holy Spirit, too. Are we looking at Him every day thinking we are just looking at the sky? If God can create worlds and universes with a breath, nothing is beyond His abilities. He shared His spirit with us. He resides inside of us our entire lives. He heals people and other living creatures while managing all of His other activities. Is anything outside of His abilities? No— nothing is.

7

CRAZY AND STRANGE
OCCURRENCES AFTER AN NDE

U
NBEKNOWNST TO GAVIN AND myself, in addition to what I've already shared about the allergy that caused me to wear a face mask, many developments complicated our lives even more (though they're typical occurrences for those who've had an NDE). Given my history of seeking help from doctors regarding the car accident, electrical shocks, and the ambush makeover, who was going to believe me now when life got more crazy and strange?

One of the common—and problematic—aftereffects of an NDE is the development of sleep disorders. After being saved by an invisible angel or God during the car accident, I didn't need as much sleep, but now, after being in the presence of God,

Jesus, and seeing who the Holy Spirit was, I seemed revved up with energy and had an even worse time sleeping.

I was so tired at times I felt like I could flop on the bed and be out like a light, but instead, as soon as I would lie down, that inner light that should have gone out came on brighter than ever. It felt like my inner being was being strengthened or revived through a spiritual quickening when I would lie down to sleep.

Another common aftereffect of an NDE are malfunctions of electrical equipment, light bulbs, and other appliances around an experiencer.

Whether or not this electrical phenomena caused my insomnia, I don't know, but in my view, when an NDEr is in the presence of the ultimate source of all energy—God— their energetic system becomes super-charged beyond what the physical body can readily assimilate. Consequently, it can take years to adapt to this enhanced energetic charge, if one can ever adjust to it at all.

Among the strange electrical phenomenon that really kicked into gear after my third NDE was the draining of batteries. P.M.H. Atwater's studies show that the electromagnetic field around an NDEr not only causes electrical malfunctions it typically drains batteries that are in close proximity to their body—most often the wristwatch.[10]

For example, I'd always worn a wristwatch, but after my third NDE, my watch batteries kept dying. At first, I replaced the battery, but that one soon died, too—as did the next and the one after that. We resorted to buying the best batteries on

---

[10] Atwater, P. *Dying to Know You.* Faber, VA: Rainbow Ridge Book LLC, 2014. E-book.

the market, but they also stopped working after a short time. I had some lovely dress watches that I didn't wear every day, and when I started wearing them, they stopped working as well.

Gavin and I concluded that the world just wasn't making quality products anymore, so I went shopping for a wind-up watch, but all I could find was a pocket watch. It was awkward fumbling in my pocket each time I wanted to check the time. I ended up having a jewelry box full of watches that didn't work.

After the living room addition was completed, the electrical phenomena persisted in the wee hours of the morning—the electrically-related weirdness seemed more prominent because it was so quiet. For example, the television or radio came on by themselves, or a light would snap and blow itself out.

One night, I shuffled myself out of bed, with sleep still in my eyes, to get a drink of water. As I walked past the open bedroom doorway, the television in the living room turned on by itself with a snowy picture. I tried to turn it off, to no avail, so Gavin came out to help. He studied the connections and was confounded as to why it happened. I was not aware that my power-charged energy and unobstructed view of the television was causing the electrical malfunction.

But this craziness was not limited to nighttime. During the day, if I was busy and rushing about, sometimes the telephone rang but no one was on the line. I believe this happened during the daytime because I was more revved up with energy than I was at night before I tried to go to bed.

When the phantom telephone phenomenon first started, I was still married to Gavin. Not yet attributing it to my NDE electrical phenomena, eventually I got irritated. In fact, I got downright suspicious! Did Gavin have a girlfriend who was calling and hanging up when I answered? Some of the calls came from New York, others from the Caribbean. I checked caller ID and immediately called the number back, ready to confront the threat to my marriage.

I connected not to a person, but to that awful buzz-tone and a recording: *We're sorry; you have reached a number that has been disconnected or is no longer in service. If you have reached this recording in error, please check the number and try your call again.*

You've got to be kidding me! What are the chances? How could this be happening? Of course, none of it made sense at the time, but clearly, as NDErs, our energy sets off or interrupts electrical charges.

This phenomenon was also demonstrated by a strange occurrence in the yard of our ranch house. The electrical company had placed an electrical pole on the north side of the house, with a new light that came on at dusk, just like a street light. The new pole accommodated the updated electrical needs for the new living room addition that we were planning, and the light was a great way to brighten up the yard at night.

We both noticed when returning to the house well after the sun disappeared, the new yard light would be flickering. When it was placed there it worked correctly, but now for some unknown reason it wasn't. I thought, *We should call to have it repaired*, but I kept forgetting it once the door closed behind us for the evening. Before my NDE, the light came on steadily when we were out after dark. After my NDE, the light flickered whenever I was outside. When

I was inside the house and peeked out I noticed it shone steadily, without a flicker. At the time, I didn't suspect that the energy I emitted was causing the anomaly, or that the house blocked my energy field when I was inside.

After Gavin and I separated, I asked him, "Did you ever get the light on the pole fixed?"

"Not necessary," Gavin replied. "It's working fine."

Later in life, I found out while reading P.M.H. Atwater's book *Dying To Know You*, that in addition to the aftereffects I'm sharing with you, that the divorce rate between an NDEr and their spouse is uncommonly high. Atwater's study of 3,000 adult NDErs showed that seventy-two to seventy-seven percent of NDErs got divorced within the first ten years of their NDE episode.[11] In broad terms, NDErs' marriages fail because their spouse claimed that the person they married was gone, replaced by someone they didn't know. Similar to two caterpillars who have shared a life, but suddenly one transforms into a butterfly, leaving the other wondering where they've vanished to. Or in my case, God needed me to be in a different place and situation to help my son Curt.

I also found out that another common aftereffect that takes place with an NDEr is a name change. In my case, all of my young life, friends and family called me Jan. But after my third NDE, I changed so much that the name Jan no longer seemed to fit, so I started introducing myself by my birth name, Janet. To me, "Jan" was a different person. This may seem like a subtle change, but it was a very significant one to me.

---

[11] Atwater, P. *Dying to Know You*. Faber, VA: Rainbow Ridge Book LLC, 2014. E-book.

During this same period, Gavin bought me my first cell phone. The cell also was not convenient to carry—it was either in my purse or pocket where I couldn't hear it or access it quickly. As I'd done many times in my past, I went to bed to try and solve the conundrum, and I dreamt of an idea.

Below is a drawing of the decorative cell phone, keychains, necklace, and pocket bobs I created to make telephone and watch access easy. They were handy for keys, whistles, pill boxes, cameras, and protective sprays as well—anything you wanted to bring along with you.

Figure 8 (left) My invention that came about due to the problem of not being able to wear a watch.

Figure 9 (right) The brochure I created for the invention.

The accessory that clipped each item to the necklace was detachable so the jewelry could be worn separately. Eventually, I patented the idea—I called it "The Bring Along."

Gavin and I took "The Bring Along" to an invention convention in hopes of selling the idea. Two businesses were interested in selling my product, but they wanted it manufactured and ready for market. I discovered that I needed a $100,000 investment minimum to start, and I didn't have that kind of money.

My "Bring Along" didn't find its place amongst the many brilliant convenience-gadgets you can buy in our modern world, but it did solve my personal dilemma.

I have experienced the rewards of being open to divine guidance in my dreams. This idea must have hung in the heavenly ethers, ready for anyone who would take it and develop it, because similar devices came on the market shortly afterward.

Many people have thought my inspirational dream was just a coincidence, but I have solved many problems during dream time. It's not only me who believes that God uses the openness of people's minds during sleep to communicate; for example, you will find dream visions referred to in the Bible. Here are just some of the Biblical verses that refer to messages coming in dreams: Genesis 41:1-7; Genesis 46:2; Judges 7:13-15; 1 Samuel 3:2-15; Daniel 2:28-29. Divine messages come through to us easily at night because while we're sleeping, our ego is sleeping too, so it cannot put up its usual roadblocks of doubt and fear.

Two years later, I was carrying the cell phone on my necklace and the electrical phenomena persisted. I was frustrated and at my wits end because the charge on the cell phone kept depleting. I didn't know the proximity of the cell phone to my body was draining it, just like my wrist watches. The phone was not that old, so I went to the carrier for an answer. They could not explain it and suggested I purchase a bigger battery that held twice the charge. Now, cell phones no longer have the same little hole for the attachment, so I carry my phone in my purse so it lasts longer (or I'm coming to terms with the energy).

Another aftereffect that we weren't aware of was that NDErs come back loving others unconditionally. I'm sure this was because of the message that was imbued into our entire being that "love is the only thing that matters." We don't go on a love fest with everyone we meet or see; rather, we're just more compassionate and caring than we were previously. This tends to leave loved ones and family members wondering what's going on.

Years later, more focus came to the surface from these curious senses I acquired. I could sense the emotions of individuals, but now I found, when I sat quietly in a calm environment, I could see in my mind's eye what a person's aura system looked like. I learned what the colors represented about the core being of the person. I could look at a picture or hold an object of a person whom I didn't know, and I could conclude a great deal about that person by focusing on their energy system.

I believe I picked this gift up when, during the last NDE, I became one with the Living Light and the colors. Remember how I described I could feel the colors from the light even though I couldn't see them?

Like many other NDErs, I continue to have contact with heavenly beings. One particular instance helped me realize monetary wealth is not important. The divorce now final, I had been waiting for the ranch to sell so I could make plans, but at the time, the ranch still hadn't sold because the market was depressed, so the majority of my money was tied up. I was waiting for the ranch to sell so I could make my move back to Colorado. It was at that moment, while I stood in my parent's Boise living room, I thought about how happy I was being surrounded by the people who loved me unconditionally, even though I didn't have a lot of money.

I thought to myself, *If I never have anything in my life ever again, I'll be joyful if I'm surrounded by the people who love me.* Jesus appeared briefly with a simple nod and smile on His face, showing His approval of my recognition of the importance of love instead of monetary wealth. Then He was gone.

It's interesting to note that each time I had a revelation on how He works in our lives and had the thought, *Oh, that's what He's showing me!*, Jesus showed up, smiled, nodded His head, or gave me another affirmation, and was gone.

About two or three weeks after that realization and encounter with Jesus, I received a call. Gavin wanted to let me know there was a significant deposit of oil discovered under our property. At that moment, I remembered the vision of the oil rig during the conveyance of universal knowledge. God knew this was going to happen and it did. The property we purchased was referred to as a Railroad Parcel, which meant we didn't own the minerals under it. The railroad company was the holder of the mineral deposits, but as a kind gesture they gave a tiny percentage to the surface owner.

The oil wells on the property had not done much in the past years, but this was different. The checks started coming in monthly, which were significant, and they were predicted to go on for approximately thirty years. It was as if God knew when I was going to have the realization that material wealth wasn't what made us happy but love did, and now He was rewarding me for the thought. Isn't it amazing how He works?

Another encounter I had with Jesus or God was when my newfound intuition flowed into my dream time, where I, in spirit form, traveled the universe to experience spirit lessons. I have, for example, been whisked up beyond the veil to the whiteness of heaven for a review of what I have learned about judgment. These nightly sojourns to the netherworld used to surprise me, but now I welcome the opportunity to spend time learning more about my spiritual development.

During one of these heavenly meetings, I had an encounter with God or Jesus (I don't know for sure which because He wouldn't let me see His face). Interestingly, not seeing God's face is in the Bible, too, when God spoke to Moses. This was how God told Moses he will never be seen:

> "The LORD replied, 'I will make all my good-ness pass before you ... But you may not look directly at my face, for no one may see me and live.' The LORD continued, 'Stand here on this rock beside me. As my glorious presence passes by, I will put you in the cleft of the rock and cover you with my hand until I have passed. Then I will remove my hand, and you will see me from behind. But my face will not be seen.'"
> (Exodus 33:19-23 NLT)

While I stood with the LORD, I saw His white robe, and this time it went down to His knees. It was tied at the waist with a rope, and I could see His knees, calves, and feet. I can only describe this spiritual being's legs as being much larger and more muscular than that of the spiritual being who appeared before me in the NDE where I couldn't breathe. They were thick and gave me the distinct sense that they were the legs of a giant.

He wore sandals and His feet were equally massive. We had been talking far out in space. He (I believe it was God) stood to my left, and as we floated among the stars, we looked down on earth. It was far enough away that it appeared to be the size of a basketball and I could see all of it easily. I'll never forget the mystic colors and the sense of universal connection to everything. Even the space that appeared to be empty was in fact filled, but with a lesser density.

I asked God what "it" was all about, and while He raised His fully extended right arm, palm up into the air, He said, "Behold." Suddenly, I saw streaks of light flying in different directions, and each one sounded like Luke Skywalker's lightsaber being swung through the air. The streaks of light created lines, and I knew they were going to the many worlds and dimensions that God has created. I had no doubt that humans were not the only life form He created, and each level was for a specific purpose.

I understood and said, "Oh, I get it! It's all about math."

And He said, "Yes."

In that moment, I understood that God is the King of

Quantum Theory, which is a theory of modern physics that explains the behavior of matter and energy, not only at the atomic level but at the subatomic level. Quantum Theory was first introduced by Max Planck, a physicist working in the early 1900's, using a mathematical equation.[12]

I believe that not only did God use quantum mechanics to create the universe, but that God is Quantum Theory in its entirety. Quantum Theory (even though it didn't have a name in those days) is what I believe Paul is referring to when he said:

> "Christ is the one through whom God created everything in heaven and earth. He [God] created things we can see and the things we cannot see—kings, kingdoms, rulers, and authorities. Everything has been created through him and for him. He existed before everything else began, and he holds all creation together." (Colossians 1:16-17 NLT)

Now that you know more about the typical aftereffects of NDEs and STEs, perhaps you can appreciate how profound— and life-changing—such experiences can be for NDErs, their spouses, and their families.

---

[12] Rouse, M. "Quantum Theory." *WhatIs*. Accessed February 6, 2018. http://whatis.techtarget.com/definition/quantum-theory

8
THE REASON I STAYED

LET'S TURN THE CLOCK back to the time when the divorce was being finalized. I moved to my parent's home in Boise, Idaho, taking me over 800 miles away from my three children. They were in their twenties, with lives of their own, so I couldn't pack them up and take them with me.

Two years later, I was still in Idaho. Our Colorado ranch was on the market, but it hadn't sold. My son Phillip was living and working in Denver, and Curt and Gina were in northern Colorado.

I was deeply moved when my middle son, Curt, called and asked if I would move back to Colorado and share an apartment with him. God had laid it in his heart to get me back to Colorado. What Curt didn't know was that God did this for a reason. I'd seen a holographic image of Curt during my third

NDE, and this request that I happily accepted was going to put me in the right place at the right time for whatever was about to happen. Isn't that remarkable?

It's incredible to me that God has broader plans for our lives, which is laid out in Psalm 32:8: "The LORD says, '"I will make you wise and show you where to go. I will guide you and watch over you"' (NLT).

I often thought about that holographic image I saw of Curt as a handsome, young man. It wasn't easy, waiting and wondering about how his trials would unfold. Would it be soon? Would the event happen to him, or would it be a sorrowful time for him enduring the suffering of a loved one? As it turned out, not long after I returned to Colorado, Curt's lesson presented itself.

We lived in a college town, and the authorities were strict about driving under the influence. One night after Curt had been out partying, he left a club where he enjoyed country dancing and headed for home. He was pulled over and blew over the limit. He lost his license, was put on probation, and had to attend DUI classes.

One day, I stood in the living/dining room area of the apartment we shared, with my son in the hallway facing his bedroom door. Calmly, I asked him why I hadn't heard about or driven him to any of his required meetings lately.

Curt turned to look at me and said he wasn't going, and then he turned his head back toward his bedroom. Now looking into his room, he replied with a sense of hopelessness: "Because my probation officer doesn't like me. I just don't see any light at the end of the tunnel."

"Well," I said to him, "he won't like you unless you start doing what you're supposed to do. To see any light at the end of the tunnel, you have to start somewhere."

As Curt stood there, I saw a light bulb turn on over his head, just like that old roast beef sandwich commercial where the company logo that looks like a cowboy hat appeared over the actor's head while he thought of the delicious fast food.

Curt got it.

I told Curt I would take him everywhere he needed to go. "Just ask, and I'll be there," I said. He took the initiative and bought a bike to get to work. He set up an appointment with his probation officer and we went together.

For a long time, the probation officer sized us both up as we sat in his office. Then, finally, he said, "Well, what's going on with you?"

Curt answered, "I'm sorry, and I would like to know what I need to do to get into your good graces."

That was the turning point in Curt's life that I'd needed to stay for. My words literally "turned the light on" in his head, and he began his journey back to being the incredible person he is today. I don't know precisely what might have happened in Curt's life if I hadn't been there for him, but I do know he would have gone down a different, destructive path.

I felt that, viscerally, during my NDE. I realized that when Curt told me he couldn't see the light at the end of the tunnel, those words were God's slick way of communicating to me that this was the event I'd stayed for. Me being there, saying those words, and supporting him helped Curt embrace and learn his life's lesson. By the end of Curt's classes, he looked like the holographic image I saw in my NDE so many years ago.

Our lessons in life are essential for our soul's growth, even though we might not like learning them. We mustn't let our difficulties define us—we just have to see them as stepping stones to maturity. When you make a mistake, which ones do you remember most? Is it the silly mistakes, or the hard, embarrassing errors that stick out in your mind?

These are the mistakes that can help you advance the most. When you overcome them, you develop personal courage, power, and resilience. Don't dwell on your mistakes and don't let your past hold you back. Persevere and be proud, knowing that you have mastered that lesson. Check it off your list and move forward boldly into your bright future.

As you walk your life's path, always remember that God has your back. When you are feeling like your challenges are too difficult for you to face alone, or you are in trouble, just ask for God's help and He will guide you. Remember, He already knows what you need because He's inside of you. What Curt may not have known, but God did, the probation officer that sat across from us that day in his office ended up being an advocate that supported Curt in many ways. This proves that sincerity, perseverance, and follow-through make a difference in all aspects or our lives.

Curt, one day after hunting with friends, shared a story about something that happened that day. Curt told it like this: They walked through the mountain forest seeking their prey, trying to keep each other in sight. Curt said he got separated from the group, and as he walked, he didn't realize he was getting farther away. Finally, he came upon a stream and realized he was lost. He told me he thought, *What should I do?* He told me he went into survival mode, looking at the creek and thinking: *I accidentally left my water bottle somewhere along the way. At least I'll have water to drink.*

Curt explained, having already shot off his call for help with no response, that he wondered which direction he should go, but he thought: *it all looks the same. What if I go in the wrong direction and get lost even worse than I already am?*

So he sat on a tree stump for quite some time, trying to decide what to do until he heard a rustling in the brush. Suddenly on high alert, Curt didn't know what to expect when a one-armed man with a rifle came through the bushes.

"Are you lost, son?" the man asked.

Curt replied, "Yes, I am."

The man told him to go in a certain direction and exactly how far, explaining he would find his group shortly.

As he unlaced his boots and continued telling me his story, Curt said, "I did as he told me and it led me back to my friends. The strange thing is, Mom, that he didn't even ask me what group I was with." He cocked his head and gave me a serious look. "I think he was an angel, Mom."

I also trust that the man was an angel, if not God himself, appearing in a way that would be comfortable for Curt. Otherwise the man wouldn't have known Curt was lost before he entered the clearing. This reminded me of the Bible verse Hebrews 13:2, that tells us to "remember to welcome strangers, because some who have done this have welcomed angels without knowing it" (NCV). And how cool is it that the one-armed man called him "son"? I'll let you decide if Curt saw an angel or God.

Another important lesson I've learned is to not feel remorseful or guilty about my mistakes—I have done the best I could with what I knew at the time. Admit an error, be vulnerable, and let people get to know the real you. Remember, the people who play parts in our lessons have agreed, at a soul level, to help us. Some of the most challenging people in our lives are our most noteworthy advocates on the other side. It can be hard to swallow, but this is true nonetheless.

Curt is an excellent example of how adversity can be overcome if you set your mind to it. It took several years for him to see the light at the end of the tunnel, but he persevered and broke through. I'm proud of him. Today, he's a brilliant, caring, fun, compassionate, and dependable man, as well as a well-respected supervisor at a great company. He has a beautiful daughter and a wonderful life. He set his mind to getting everything right—and he did it.

When you are presented with obstacles in your life, don't stand in your own way. Use your inner wisdom. What do you want? What's blocking you? Is it your own fear? Remember, with God's help, anything is possible. Remember, too, that maybe you are not getting what you want in life because God has something better in mind for you.

If what you really want is to be your best self, you must do your part and take the necessary steps—take classes, read books, and seek assistance. There is an abundant amount of help available out there to help you achieve your dreams—you just have to find it.

Remember to smile and let the world in. A smile is inviting. I consciously made the decision to smile wherever I went, and it changed everything. People started smiling back and saying hello. It opened up my world.

9
MY BROTHER'S FUNERAL
Spirit In Attendance

Our family hub that was initially in Iowa during my childhood is now in Idaho, where our parents live. My brother Doug and sister Diane also live in that area. Life took my brother Dennis—Doug's twin—to Oregon and me to Colorado. Our parent's home was a central gathering point, and we tried to schedule our family vacations in Idaho so we could all get together.

Curt had gotten married and started a family. The ranch had still not sold, and my oldest son Phillip had, in the interim, purchased a three-bedroom fixer-upper home in a nearby Colorado town. It was only him living in the house, so he asked me to come live with him, and I helped him with the home improvements.

One year on July 14th, I received a call from my sister-in-law Judy, Dennis' wife. They had left earlier that day to spend a week visiting my mom and dad, Doug, Diane and all of their families. I saw on my call display that Judy was calling, and I answered with a chipper voice—Judy is delightful, easy, and fun to talk to. I knew they were still on the road, so I thought she was calling to update me on their adventure.

Judy's voice, however, was soft and guarded. My dad had just called her with tragic news which she passed on to me: Doug had had a fatal heart attack that morning. Judy and Dennis had pulled over to the side of the highway to gather their composure, and to comfort one another. So Dennis could have some time to himself, Judy was making the family calls.

Doug was sixty-one, young by today's standards, and he had not been ill, so his death was a surprise. He'd been helping my mom, in her eighties, to change the bed sheets, anticipating Dennis and Judy's arrival. Doug was on the side of the bed next to the window, in a narrow gap that was hard for my mom to maneuver into. He'd suddenly clutched his heart, gasped for air, and fallen between the bed and the wall, downed by a massive heart attack.

My smile was instantly wiped from my face. I felt like a doe caught in headlights, frozen and too powerless to move. Finally, I lowered my head, my shoulders slumped, and my face went blank in shock at the tragic news. I steadied myself by leaning on the desk as Judy told me my mom and dad were calling from the hospital, and told us all hope was gone. I felt as if I was out-of-body and that this was happening to someone else. But I was wrong—it was true.

Later I found out when the heart attack occurred, my mom called my dad, but they couldn't reach Doug. The bed was too big for them to move and a dresser limited their access. I was told my mom yelled, "We're losing him!" and my dad ran as fast as his eighty-year-old legs would carry him to the neighbor's house for help.

We were all devastated and in a state of shock. I had to buy a plane ticket to get to Idaho fast. I started shuffling through papers on my desk, not sure of what I was looking for. Then the grief hit me, and I leaned against the desk and sobbed. While the knowledge I'd acquired from my NDEs was of some help, losing Doug was hard. I hoped that my NDEs and the wisdom I'd gained from them might help my parents, even if their pain was current and raw. I was hopeful, but could anyone ease the pain of losing a child?

My initial response was to drop everything and fly out that night to be there for my parents and stay for a few weeks to help. But coordinating a flight and a ride to the airport was not so easy. First I called my children, then I called the airlines to check flights to Boise. After figuring out my flight options, I chose to leave first thing the next morning. This gave me time to pack for a more extended stay.

In times of death, it has long been customary as part of the bereavement process for family and friends to visit their loved one at the mortuary. This provides an opportunity to say good-bye and to see the departed loved one, one last time. My dad had been to the mortuary several times, but my mom couldn't bring herself to go.

She saw Doug at the hospital after the tragic event. My mom said that he "just seemed to be sleeping" and that's how she preferred to remember him. She just sat in her recliner, hand on her forehead, in a state of pure grief. My heart ached not only for the loss of my brother, but for everyone's suffering, since they didn't know the true beauty of indescribable love and peace Doug was now experiencing.

As soon as I got to Boise, I wanted to pay my respects to Doug and get one last glimpse of him. I arrived late in the afternoon and the next day was my last opportunity, so I went straight to the mortuary when I got up. He looked great, like the Doug I knew, sleeping peacefully. I was sad, of course, knowing this was the last time I would see him. I wondered what he thought of me. Had I been a good sister? Did I fail in some way?

As he lay there before me, I didn't want to lose that last moment to express my love for him. I caressed his face, kind of clumsily. I hadn't touched a dead body before, and how do you caress your brother's face? We'd always hugged or rested our hands on each other's shoulders as gestures of love, but I'd never touched either of my brother's faces.

With love and a little curiosity, I gently ran my fingers up and down Doug's face in a figure-eight motion. I covered his face and eyes with gentle kisses and said my goodbyes. I knew he was probably around and would feel the love I had for him in my heart. I knew how happy he must be, being held in the loving arms of God. The memory of the pure love and bliss from my last near-death experience was still fresh in my mind (as it is to this day).

That night, I was caught up in a more complete description of the tragedy in an unusual way. My mom was well known for talking in her sleep, since she was depressed, grieving, and exhausted when she went to bed. I was in the extra bedroom near the kitchen. Even though it was located at the opposite end of the house, the hallway created a funnel of sound so any conversation could be heard through the open door of my room.

In the wee hours of morning, I heard her anguished screams of desperation. It was heart-wrenching, and tears came to my eyes with sorrow, not only for my brother, but for my mom and dad, too. I was caught up in the event that I had only heard bits and pieces of so far. As my mom dreamt, I heard her cry out, "Dick! Dick! Help! We're losing him! We're losing him! Hurry! Hurry!"

I believe this must have been when my dad hurried in from the other room and tried to gain access to Doug, but to no avail. Then I heard her desperate cry, "Get Steve! Hurry!", which was when my dad ran as fast as he could next door for help. The neighbor Steve was home and sprinted to my mom and dad's house. He flew into the room, picked up the massive bed, and moved it to gain access to Doug. The EMTs soon arrived and continued life-saving measures in hopes of reviving Doug on the way to the hospital, but he didn't make it. Then I heard her cries of sorrow as her dream seemed to end.

While we were planning Doug's funeral, my sister Diane went home each night to get some rest. One evening, she decided to process her grief by drawing a picture of Doug. Diane went to her computer to find a photo of him. She had a

"Doug" folder, containing pictures of him at celebrations and other events. She clicked on the folder icon, expecting to see the usual spread of small photos in the catalog. Instead, a poem called "When Tomorrow Starts Without Me" popped up on the screen.

Diane had never seen the poem before, so she asked around to see if anyone in her family had anything to do with the poem appearing on her computer. No one knew the poem or where it had come from. Diane realized it had to be a message from Doug, so she called us. She copied the poem and brought it to my mom and dad's the next day.

Another odd thing was that the message in Diane's computer was not the entire poem. It was as if Doug picked just the right verses of David M. Romano's long poem "When Tomorrow Starts Without Me"[13] to convey his message. The original poem has thirty-four lines—Doug's communication contained only eight, four which are quoted here:

When tomorrow starts without me, and I'm not here to see;

If the sun should rise and find your eyes,
filled with tears for me;
I wish so much you wouldn't cry
the way you did today,
While thinking of the many things,
we didn't get to say.

---

[13] Romano, David. "When Tomorrow Starts Without Me." In Canfield, J., Hansen, M., & Kirberger, K. *Chicken Soup for the Soul on Tough Stuff.* Cos Cob, Connecticut: Chicken Soup for the Soul Publishing, 2012.

Doug ended his message with, "Don't think we're far apart."

In honor of Doug, Judy and I put together a picture board, arranging photographs of Doug and Dennis, the fraternal twins, with shots of Doug playing hockey with his nephew and niece when they were children. We laid out a series of photos of Doug's life in a progression of memorable experiences.

Family, friends, and coworkers showed up en masse for Doug's funeral. We placed a framed picture of Doug, some flowers, and an urn containing his ashes on a table. We set a beautiful flower arrangement with a cross at the base of the table. It looked great, and we knew Doug would have liked it.

I knew Doug's service would be remembered for a long time, and I wanted to catch it on film to keep those memories vivid, so I took pictures. Since I was a member of the family, I felt that I was the only person who could really take pictures without anyone getting offended. Of course, I asked my parents ahead of time just in case, and they agreed it was okay.

Doug was well-loved by colleagues, family, and friends. We received many heartfelt condolences after he passed. One couple wrote to say that Doug was such a great person, they had named their son after him—something he'd never shared with us. Others talked about all his great personality traits, among them, how kind and funny he was.

Often, when Doug wanted to be funny, he'd step into the living room in a Superman stance. We all agreed that each time he did this, we could hear the music that played when Superman was on his way to save someone. We chuckled every time.

After the funeral, I downloaded the pictures I'd taken during the service from my camera. As we looked at them, Judy and I noticed an anomaly—there was a good-sized orb in one photo, right above Doug's picture. At the moment I'd snapped the shot, the pastor had been giving a blessing. She had her right arm raised and was using her fingers to make the shape of the cross. I remembered all of the orbs I saw during my NDEs and how, once my spirit had come together during my third NDE, I felt like an orb as well. When I saw that orb, I knew that Doug had attended his own funeral.

A week after the funeral, Dennis and his family needed to return to Oregon. They left early and didn't want to wake anyone, so they were quiet. As they got ready to go, I was in the midst of "a dream-state vision." While my body laid in bed, my spirit was taken up to heaven, where I found myself standing in a celestial white room. Doug appeared in the doorway, dressed in white.

He looked perfect. His persona was more commanding than it was in the earthly realm, and he exuded a sense of peacefulness, confidence, and love that is hard to describe, but is the common state of being on the other side. With just a thought, we were in each other's arms—it was as if we floated toward each other with an intention to embrace.

I felt his body against mine just like it happened in the physical world, and I was ecstatic to see him. While we embraced, he rubbed my back in the exact "figure-eight" motion I used when I caressed his face at the funeral home. I felt the figure-eight clearly and knew he was letting me know he'd been there that day, at the funeral home.

Telepathically, I exclaimed, *You were there! You saw me!*

Suddenly, Doug started to back away. I knew he was leaving, so I reached for him in desperation, calling out, "No, don't go! Don't go, Doug!" He smiled and moved further back. Then, he vanished.

I woke up in tears, knowing Doug had just said goodbye. I had to recover quickly since Dennis and his family were ready to leave. I joined my parents to share our goodbyes. I didn't tell anyone what had happened—how could I have explained it?

After Dennis and Judy had returned to Oregon, Judy decided to finish reading a book she'd already started, *Proof of Heaven*[14] by Dr. Eben Alexander[15]. One day she called, exclaiming, "You won't believe what I just found in the book I was reading!"

Dr. Eben Alexander spent over twenty-five years as an academic neurosurgeon, including fifteen years at the Brigham and Women's Hospital, the Children's Hospital, and Harvard Medical School in Boston. Dr. Alexander thought he had a good idea of how the brain generates consciousness, mind, and spirit.[14] [15] At least, he thought so until he contracted a rare, mysterious bacterial infection—meningoencephalitis— and found himself journeying through an afterlife he previously believed didn't exist.

Judy told me she'd found the same poem that had unexplainably popped up on Diane's computer. In Chapter 35 of his book, Dr. Alexander, who was adopted as a newborn and raised by loving adoptive parents, shares that the lines to "When Tomorrow Starts Without Me" had been affixed to a picture of his birth sister, which was given to him four months after he was released from the hospital.

---

[14] Alexander, E. M. *Proof of Heaven.* New York: Simon & Schuster, 2012.
[15] "Dr. Eben Alexander III MD." *Eben Alexander.* Accessed November 8, 2017. http://ebenalexander.com/about/

That picture was significant to Dr. Alexander because he'd spent time with his birth sister during his near-death experience in the hospital. His birth sister had died before he was reunited with his birth family and he'd never seen her photo until after his NDE. He recognized that his sister was unquestionably the beautiful woman who had come to greet him riding upon a butterfly.

I was still at my mom and dad's a day or two later when Gina called from Denver. Gina never called from work, but she was excited. She wanted to tell me she was sure she'd had a message from Doug. A coworker had brought her a poem which they just felt they were supposed to give to her.

"Wait!" I said. "Was it called 'When Tomorrow Starts Without Me'?"

"How did you know?" she exclaimed.

I told her about both Diane and Judy receiving the same poem.

To sum all of this up, Doug left behind three siblings when he transitioned to the other side: Dennis, Diane, and me. Diane got the poem's most meaningful lines on her computer first. Judy got this same poem from Dr. Alexander's book. Gina received the poem from a friend on behalf of our family. Doug made sure that all three of his siblings got the same beautiful message.

Each of the three times this poem came to a member of our family, we shared the message with our parents. That a poem none of us had ever heard of came to us three separate times within the first three weeks after Doug's death is indeed not just a coincidence—that is the power of the heavenly realm.

It's comforting to realize the vision of Doug during my allergy-induced NDE was a confirmation Doug would be joining God in the heavenly realm in the near future, and He also wanted us to know we are eternal beings who transition at just the right time.

10

THE BUILDING, THE WORD NAMASTE, AND THE SOUL PAINTING

ABOUT TEN MONTHS AFTER Doug passed away, I went through emails on my computer. I'd previously signed up to receive vouchers from a coupon website that was all the rage. I scrolled through their offerings for deals on restaurants and beauty salons and suddenly, a coupon caught my interest: fifty percent off something called a "soul painting." It was being offered by an artist named Teresa Dunwell from the Living Works Studio.[16]

I'd never heard of a soul painting, but since I'd been shown my soul in my NDE, I thought it would be fun to see what

---

[16] Dunwell, T., *Living Works Studio*. Accessed March 6, 2018. http://livingworksstudio.com

an artist could create. I called Gina to see if she would like to get one of these paintings done, too. The artist was in a town forty-five minutes away, so we decided to make a day of it, and stopped for lunch before the meeting.

I called to make the appointment and got a voicemail recording. I left my first name and my phone number. The next morning, still in a dream-state, I noticed I was in the same celestial white room I had been in before. On the verge of waking, I heard a gentle female voice say, "Namaste" and at that instant, I was awakened by the ringing telephone. It was the soul painter, Teresa, returning my call. We set up a weekend appointment.

I called Gina to tell her the appointment time, and I shared with her about the "Namaste" I'd heard the moment the telephone rang. At the time, neither of us knew what "Namaste" meant, and we both wondered if the artist prayed before calling. Had I somehow picked up on it?

On the day of the appointment, Gina and I had lunch and drove to Teresa's office that seemed eerily familiar to a vision I was shown while in God's embrace. Teresa directed us down a walkway and told us she'd join us in a moment. Upon entering the waiting room, right there on a door was a sign that read, "Namaste." I gasped, pointed at the sign, and whispered, "Gina, there it is!"

When she joined us, I asked Teresa what namaste meant. "It means my spirit honors your spirit," she replied. How amazing is that?

"Do you say a prayer before returning calls?" I asked.

"Sometimes, but not all of the time," Teresa said.

I don't know if it was Teresa's voice I'd heard that morning, but someone had wanted me to come to appreciate that word. Perhaps while I was in the celestial white dimension, I was reading the heavenly records and this was the moment in time God had shown me what was preordained to occur.

We eagerly entered Teresa's pleasant office. Her well-used art supplies were neatly organized next to and on a table. Gina said I should go first, so I took the chair across from where Teresa's art supplies were laid out. Teresa took a seat at the table across from me so we were face-to-face and I could see what she was painting. *This is going to be fun,* I thought.

When I'd set up the appointment, I didn't ask what a soul painting was, so I thought Teresa was going to paint what our souls looked like. If she were authentic, I thought, she'd depict my soul as being blue because, in my NDE, I'd seen my brilliant, sky-blue soul lifting out of my body.

Teresa asked if we knew what a soul painting was about. She explained that with the client's permission, she said a prayer for a message that was true, accurate, and for the highest good. She then connected her senses to the heavenly chronicles in which all of history is recorded. Through prayer, Teresa said, the gatekeeper of the holy records shared with her, through visions imprinted upon her mind's eye, what to paint. The final painting was something the gatekeeper of the heavenly records wanted to verify for the person, or for something he wanted the person to know.

As Teresa painted, she explained the colors that the gatekeeper was showing her. Each color meant something about the quality of their core person. For instance, pink represented a loving nature, orange represented creativity, and purple represented intuitive strength. Every part of the painting had some kind of meaning, and the final depiction was meaningful as well.

Teresa started painting, telling me that the keeper of the records was showing her circles. "Interesting," she said. The guardian of the records showed her where on the paper to draw the circles. As she continued, she came over to me periodically to "feel the energy" around my body.

She painted a line here and a line there with different colors. There didn't seem to be a set pattern to what she was creating. The placement of the circles and lines didn't make sense for a while, but then I started to recognize something. I didn't say anything; however, I wanted to see the final picture.

Forty-five minutes into the session, I became sure of what Teresa was painting. I fought back the tears, trying to remain composed.

I looked over at Gina. "Do you know what she's painting?" I asked.

Gina nodded. "Yes," she said. I'd explained my NDE to Gina enough times that she knew the painting was of what I'd seen during my third NDE.

The circles Teresa painted were placed on the paper in the same positions as the pin of light that had traveled, approaching where I was floating in front of Jesus. The circles were the size of the pin of light in the distance, and they grew larger and larger to reflect the increasing size of the light as it evolved into the living Light of God.

The most significant circle Teresa painted was where the Light of God was located next to Jesus. Jesus had presented the Light to me, and his right hand was slightly overlapping the tunnel when he'd said, "It's time to come home, Jan." Teresa's depiction of the scene was mind-blowing.

Teresa only painted what the gatekeeper showed her—and the message, she told us, was from Heaven and should have significance for the customer. She'd painted a part of my near-death experience! My mind was blown! I thought frantically, *I already know this happened. I already know it's important. Why are you showing me this? What am I supposed to do?*

Before she moved on to Gina's soul painting, we told Teresa the significance of what she painted and asked her who the little figure was hovering over the larger one. She explained it was a cherub angel who was looking over the larger figure.

As I wrote Teresa's explanation, I realized something else: at first I had thought that the spiritual being I saw had wings of its own, but then after the radiating light was added to the picture, I thought it was merely the light rays that gave the illusion of wings. From what Teresa painted, however, and from writing this encounter now, I believe that those wings in fact belonged to the cherub that accompanied the larger figure, like Teresa had described.

I left Teresa's studio that day shaken and wondering, *What am I supposed to do now? Why can't God just spell it out for me?*

Before the appointment, Teresa only knew my first name and phone number. At that time, she couldn't have accessed any information on the internet about me, since I didn't have a web presence. In any event, she couldn't have known about the visions I'd seen in my NDE—I'd only shared the particulars with a few family members, none of whom knew Teresa. So, what did God want me to do with this information?

One night, I contemplated that question while remembering this light in my third NDE, and realized that by sending this vision again through Teresa, God was saying that He wanted me to share my experiences, to help give peace to others. But what could I do, and how? I thought about my strengths and weaknesses. I was a quiet person, not a public speaker. I was only comfortable communicating in a one-on-one environment.

I realized my only other choice was to write a book. At that time, though my cognitive problem of connecting words and numbers had gotten better after my partial physical healing at the Miracle Crusade, I still didn't believe I could write a book—it would just be too hard. But, God wanted me to do something, and those seemed to be my only two options.

That evening, I climbed into bed and snuggled into my puffy blanket with this dilemma foremost in my thoughts. As warmth and serenity enveloped me, I thought, *If I pray about what to do and I don't get an answer, that will be my answer—I won't have to do anything.*

So, I prayed. *Dear Father in Heaven, what am I supposed to do with these experiences? Do you want me to do something with them? Should I write a book or were all of these events meant just for me? Please, tell me what to do!*

I slept soundly that night, not expecting nor really wanting an answer, but as I awoke the next morning, I heard a powerful, loving father-like voice say: "Make it about Me." At that moment, I also was shown a vision where I was speaking in front of a crowd of people. He showed me I was not only to just write a book, I was supposed to talk about it. He showed me He expected more out of me than the limitations I had considered when I was contemplating what He wanted me to do. The answer to this prayer was how this book came to be.

Throughout that day, my ego conveyed its usual negative self-talk, *See what you've got yourself into? Why did you ask? Remember that saying, "Be careful what you ask for?" Now you've done it!* But I had my answer. Now I had to figure out how to write a book, and more importantly, how to correctly express everything I had to share.

Again you might be thinking, "Really? Can this really happen? Do messages from God, Jesus, or Heaven really come during dreams?" I say yes. Dream messages are a part of numerous spiritual belief systems, and as my background is in the Western religious tradition, I've included below a couple of points in the Bible where this type of heavenly communication is conveyed.

Mary became pregnant with, Jesus, the son of God, without ever having lain with a man. Her husband-to-be, Joseph, didn't have faith in her word. Distraught, he considered calling everything off with Mary. Then Joseph had a dream:

> As he considered this, he fell asleep, and an angel of the Lord appeared to him in a dream. "Joseph, son of David," the angel said, "do not be afraid to go ahead with your marriage to Mary. For the

child within her has been conceived by the Holy Spirit. And she will have a son, and you are to name him Jesus, for he will save his people from their sins." (Matthew 1:20-21 NLT)

Another Bible verse verifying that divine dream messages can be found is 1 Kings 3:5: "That night the LORD appeared to Solomon in a dream, and God said, 'What do you want? Ask, and I'll give it to you!'" (NLT). Solomon asked for the ability to understand so he could govern his people, knowing the difference between right and wrong. God was pleased that Solomon had asked for wisdom, not material wealth or long life, so He gave Solomon what he asked for.

After my visit to Teresa's soul painting studio, I realized that I had, for a long time, placed limitations on myself because of fear and a lack of self-worth. I know that many of us do the same thing, and we do it by misinterpreting the words and intentions of others. To overcome this and get onto the path of attaining your dreams, you have to first evaluate your feelings and limitations.

Ask yourself, why do I feel this way? Who made me feel this way? Did I accept someone else's judgments about me instead of my own truth? Was there a problem within their own psyche and not mine? Could this be because they were treated this way and they don't realize how harmful their behavior is? This is why we must be mindful of our own behavior, stop the negativity within us and start spreading love and encouragement instead. What you may find is that no one can make you feel a certain way—you interpret your experiences to make your own conclusions. That may not seem like truth for you upon first consideration, but as you tap deeper into your own emotional world, you will come to discover that it is indeed true. We often take on what we're told, but it's important not to take on another person's misperceptions of both us and others.

In my case, for example, I realized that I placed my own weaknesses upon myself. Now, God asked me to challenge those weaknesses and do something I didn't think I could do. So, I stepped up and re-evaluated myself. I reflected on my NDE where I'd witnessed my soul, my personal share of the Holy Spirit. I remembered that God is always with me. He sees what I see and He experiences life with me because He lives inside of me.

I realized, too, that if I listened to my soul's guidance, I was capable of doing much more than I thought. I decided that I'd use sound wisdom and judgment, work hard, and have faith that God would place the help I needed in my path. I needed to trust Him and if it didn't happen, I thought, then He had something better planned for me.

The rest of that year passed quickly. I purchased and settled into my new home when January suddenly arrived. It was now eight months after Teresa had painted my soul painting, and I was babysitting my four-year-old granddaughter in my home. To my knowledge, my granddaughter hadn't painted with big paper, brushes, and bottles of acrylic water color, and I wanted to teach her how to use her creativity. So, I had purchased eight bottles of acrylic paint in various colors for her to mix and create new colors with.

I watched her carefully and showed her how to mix blue with red to create purple, and red with yellow to make orange. Her eyes were big with wonder. She exclaimed, "Let me do it, let me do it!" so I turned the dishful of colors and a large piece of paper over to her to experiment with.

While she mixed colors and created swirls and dots, I decided to try painting my third NDE. I'd always been waiting until I picked up better paints and paper—but that time had never come—so I thought I'd try it anyway. *I can always do a better depiction later,* I thought.

I took a moment to say a prayer. I asked God to send me an angel-artist to help guide me. I started with a circle to represent the living Light of God that had appeared next to the spirit-being. Then, I drew the figure I later recognized as Jesus, but I placed him too far to the right. His hair was too thick, and I didn't know how to create finer textured hair because, well, I'm not an artist. But after only ten minutes, I was satisfied that I'd come reasonably close to depicting what I'd seen.

Here is Teresa's soul painting and the painting I created eight months later. Unquestionably, the elements are similar.

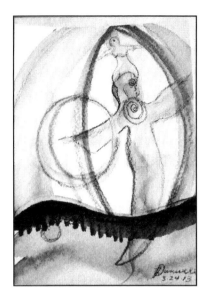

Figure 10 (left) The Soul Painting.

Figure 11 (right) Jesus from my NDE—the likenesses are unmistakable.

11

COLTON BURPO'S NDE
Confirms What I Saw

E ASTER WAS APPROACHING, AND a few days before the holiday, a movie studio released a new motion picture, based on the book *Heaven is for Real*, about a four-year-old boy, Colton Burpo, who'd had a near-death experience.[17] The film depicted Colton and his family's lives leading up to his NDE and his family's struggles around believing Colton's NDE story. It also portrayed people's true-to-life reactions to the event, and showed how unnerving a post-NDE experience can be, not only for an NDEr but also for an NDEr's family and friends.

The film depicted part of what Colton saw when he died and traveled out of his body into the heavenly realm. The efforts of

---

[17] Wallace, R. dir. *Heaven is for Real*. 2014. Culver City, CA: Sony Pictures. DVD.

the filmmakers and writers to let us see what Colton saw were remarkable. I didn't read the book until after I saw the movie. Reading the book revealed to me where the movie producers had made slight changes or where they left out information for the sake of production. As it turned out, a part of Colton's story in the book that was not included in the film related to my third NDE.

In the book, Colton and his dad (a volunteer firefighter and pastor of their church) had a conversation about the thrones in heaven. Colton described the biggest throne as the one God sat in because He was the biggest there. This reminded me of when God and I were in outer space looking down on earth, and I noticed He had the legs of a giant.

Colton also described how Jesus sat on the right side of God and the angel Gabriel sat on the left. Colton's father wondered where Colton was sitting, so he asked him. Colton told his father they brought him a little chair to sit beside the Holy Spirit. When Colton's father asked what the Holy Spirit looked like, Colton furrowed his brow and answered: "Hmm, that's kind of a hard one. . . he's kind of blue."[18]

This was significant to me because I saw my soul leave my body and it was blue, too. Both Colton's and my NDEs confirm that the spirit reveals itself as being blue in color.

Another point in the movie that brought clarity to my own NDE was what Colton saw when he stood looking at a tall birdhouse in their yard, with the cornfield in the background showing an abundant future harvest. Colton seemed to be

---

[18] Burpo, T., & Vincent, L. *Heaven is for Real* (Special Movie Edition ed.). Nashville: W Publishing Group, 2003.

reflecting on his experience, and as he stood in contemplation, a heavenly figure rose from behind the birdhouse into the sky, arms open wide.

Astonishingly, the angelic figure's stance was similar to the posture of the spiritual being in my own NDE. The overall appearance and the fact that it appeared to have wings due to the light emanation was similar to my painting, too.[19] My painting below was how the filmmakers depicted Colton's vision—an angelic figure of light, dressed in white, set against a blue sky.

Figure 12 Jesus from my NDE.

This scene is spectacular! I realize that this image was created especially for the film, but it was uncannily similar to what

[19] Wallace, R. dir. *Heaven is for Real*. 2014. Culver City, CA: Sony Pictures. DVD.

- 133 -

I saw. My painting of Jesus as pictured here, shows that Colton's experience and mine are in tandem in another way as well.

The third connection between Colton's experience and mine was that Colton saw the same Jesus I did, only I didn't see Jesus's face during my NDE. I saw Jesus's face later, when I tried something unusual after I'd learned more about a near-death experience. The image we both saw of Jesus was the same face that was painted by Akiane Kramarik when she was just eight years old. She called her portrait of Jesus *Prince of Peace*.

Kramarik started receiving heavenly visions when she was four years old, and she felt the need to express what she saw in whatever artistic medium she could get hold of. Her well-known *Prince of Peace* portrait of Jesus can be found on her website in the Akiane Gallery.[20]

Well over a year earlier, before *Heaven is for Real* was released, when I had no knowledge of Kramarik's painting, I saw Jesus a second time.

I learned during and after my NDE that we are energetic, spiritual beings, and that while earthly limitations apply to our physical bodies, the spiritual body does not have these same restrictions. On Facebook, I saw an invitation to a meditation group that was planning a worldwide meditation to heal the energy of the world and Mother Earth. The organizers believed that by sending love out into the atmosphere and around the world, a large group of meditators could raise the planet's energetic vibration. I thought, *Well, it certainly can't hurt.* I joined the group.

---

[20] Kramarik. Art Akiane LLC. *Prince of Peace*. Accessed November 8, 2017. https://akiane.com/product/prince-of-peace/

I was living with my son Phillip at the time. It was late afternoon and his work shift didn't end until 6:30, so I expected to have a couple of hours of uninterrupted time. The meditation occurred online in the privacy of our homes. When the time came, I went to my bedroom, closed the door, and slipped into the chair in front of my computer that was already queued up to the event's site. I wondered how many people were participating and where they were located, but that information wasn't displayed on the screen.

The meditation was supposed to last an hour. I relaxed, listening to the same music as the other participants. Using the power of my thoughts, I sent my energy out to encapsulate the world with positive healing energy and love. Suddenly, I saw the same light-being whom I had seen in my NDE, with his arms open wide. Instantaneously, he moved closer until I saw a good-looking man's face right in front of me. His countenance filled the entire "screen of my mind." I can't tell you why, but I knew for sure that I saw the face of Jesus—and as it turned out, He appeared to me as Kramarik had painted Him, only with longer hair and clean shaven. He obviously knew I preferred a clean-shaven face so He presented Himself in that way.

At the time of the meditation, I never saw Kramarik's work; it was over a year later that I saw her painting in the movie *Heaven is for Real.*

At the time of my third NDE, I didn't know for sure that it was Jesus I saw, since the light obscured his identity. When the meditation ended, it seemed unimportant and inconsequential that He presented himself in the same fashion as the NDE, since

I was overcome by seeing His beautiful face and shocked by the sorrow and grief He'd shared with me. That's why at the time of the meditation I didn't make the connection.

Imagine my shock when I laid eyes on Kramarik's painting and recognized her depiction as the same face I saw in the meditation! The eureka moment came when I saw a segment of the movie that depicted a spiritual figure who appeared to be Jesus raise up behind the bird house. I recalled how both the figure in the NDE and the figure in the meditation presented themselves in the same manner as that section in the film. It was at that moment I knew they were the same man in the NDE and the meditation. I'd felt the same consciousness-connection during the NDE and meditation too. I knew then that Jesus wanted me to know for sure that the face Kramarik had painted, the face I saw in the meditation, and the figure I saw in my allergy-induced NDE, were one and the same person—Jesus Himself.

In the meditation, as I viewed Jesus's beautiful face and amazing blue-green eyes. I saw a colossal tear fall from His left eye and trickle down His cheek. Then, He moved so close to me that I could only see His left eye. His tears continued to flow as He cried for what we have done to this world. I was frozen in my chair, powerless to move, as I felt His sorrow deeply, and I cried nonstop for the first half of the meditation. Then, as suddenly as it had started, the vision and experience changed.

Instead of feeling sorrow, Jesus sent a strong ray of love into my heart. It was so intense, that I felt like my heart would explode. I was so shocked and deeply moved by what had happened during that thirty minutes of divine connection, I couldn't finish the whole hour of the meditation.

Later, when I saw Kramarik's painting in the movie, I wanted to know more. I anxiously went out and bought her book, *Akiane: Her Life, Her Art, Her Poetry*.[21] In the book, Kramarik explained the deeper meanings of her painting. She said that one side—the right side—of Jesus's face that was painted in light, represented heaven while the left side painted in shadow represented the suffering on earth.

I saw the left side of Jesus's face, the side that should have been in the shadow, during the meditation, which made sense, since we were meditating to help eliminate the suffering of the world. Interestingly, however, the left side of His face was not in shadow; rather, it was in the light, which I felt was representative of His love for us in trying to bring some of the light of Heaven into the darkness and suffering of this world. That was why He zapped me with love—He loved me for having the faith to participate in that initiative.

I also found it interesting when, one day, Colton's dad asked him what an angel looks like. Colton chuckled and his description went like this: "Well, one of them looked like Grandpa Dennis, but it wasn't him."[22] Colton's description of angels having the appearance of an ordinary person supports the fact that the sumo wrestler from my childhood NDE was indeed an angelic being and even though Colton's description of angels included wings, the wings of the sumo wrestler may have very well been retracted at the time. I do know all of the beings I saw came and left as a flying ball of light.

---

[21] Kramarik, A., & Kramarik, F. *Akiane: Her Life, Her Art, Her Poetry*. Nashville: Thomas Nelson, 2006.

[22] Burpo, T., & Vincent, L. *Heaven is for Real* (Special Movie Edition ed.). Nashville: W Publishing Group, 2003.

I was so moved by Kramarik's work—her talent and vision are gifts to the world. I felt this way about the soul painting work that Teresa did for me, too. Both of these artists touched a deeper, more profound part of the human spirit, and we are blessed that they share their gifts with us.

After the soul painting Teresa did for me, and seeing the movie *Heaven is for Real*, I decided to make an appointment with a doctor who had periodically monitored my health since my "ambush makeover." I hadn't seen her for some time. On a previous occasion, we discussed my health condition that no longer included the medicines doctors had prescribed me years ago, and we agreed the doctors had misdiagnosed my condition. But, in my mind, I wonder was it Jesus's Cinderella-like touch that healed my need for those medications? However, this visit was different, I felt concerned about the message I received from Heaven via the soul painting, and the voice from Heaven that gave me the answer I didn't expect. I was having trouble sleeping. I felt I needed help and support to talk through my anxiety of what I should do.

Dr. Shelly greeted me in her office and we sat down for our meeting. She was my sounding board for most things, but I'd never told her about my NDEs. This consultation, however, was different. As we chatted, all that had recently happened was still fresh in my mind. Unexpectedly, I told her about the NDE where I couldn't breathe, and about the car accident in which the divine arms had saved me. I was concerned about sharing these things with her, and I wasn't entirely convinced I should, but I didn't have a choice: they just came out of my mouth. It was like God pushed those experiences out of me. I was stunned that it was now out there hanging in the air for someone else to see. I was exposed and vulnerable to the judgment that might come next.

I thought Dr. Shelly would think I was psychotic or hallucinating, but she didn't; in fact, she was very supportive. God must have known this would be the case. The time passed very quickly and only part of my experiences were shared, so she asked me to come back in a month so we could talk more. The month went by, and when the appointed time arrived, I decided to take my soul painting along. I thought I would disclose a little more and that once she saw that, she might understand why I felt so anxious about the future.

I told Dr. Shelly about the coupon that led me to get the soul painting done, how Teresa had said a prayer to connect with the gatekeeper of the heavenly records, and how the gatekeeper guided Teresa to paint a picture that was meaningful to the client. Then I showed Dr. Shelly the painting. She was astonished, recognizing the image as depicting the NDE I'd shared with her— like Gina did on the day the picture was painted.

"How did she do that?" Dr. Shelly asked, her mouth agape.

"I don't know," I said. "There is no way she could have known about it."

Our discussion concluded with her suggesting that I get spiritual advice from my church. I'd already called the church, but they had not yet returned my call, so I told Dr. Shelly that I'd follow up with them soon.

12

THE HOLY SPIRIT SHAKES MY SOUL WITH A MESSAGE TO TELL

O N THE WEEKEND FOLLOWING my last meeting with Dr. Shelly, there was a meeting at church that I'd signed up to attend.

I'd attended this church for quite some time, and I enjoyed the people and the atmosphere, so I was planning to become a member. Membership required participation in three "Summit Meetings," where they discussed the church and its philosophies, and helped new members find community volunteer roles if so desired. I was looking forward to the Summits.

I attended the first meeting, after which we completed an assessment similar to a personality test. Once the questions and our answers were analyzed, we were each sent a report that captured our strengths, or personal "gifts from God." This helped us know where and how we might use our strong points to serve the needs of the church and the community.

The evaluation asked us to note our personal interests—presumably, so the administrators could recommend areas of service which might best suit us and thereby keep everyone happy in their volunteer roles. It was made clear, too, that if we started volunteering and discovered that the tasks we took on didn't suit us, we could choose another area. It wasn't unusual for newcomers to try out several functions, and some people even found that volunteering was not for them, which was also fine. The questionnaire was fascinating, and I looked forward to hearing what "gifts God had given me."

I had recently called and written to my church. The church was calling for stories where God had made a difference in their life. I had sent a brief accounting to the call and offered to participate. I also wrote to the pastor for spiritual guidance and still hadn't received a call from the pastor about my submission regarding the NDE nor the guidance I requested.

The night of the second Summit arrived and, eagerly anticipating the event, I drove to church. My strengths, according to the assessment, seemed to me very accurate. Here are the top five of nineteen assessed gifts, from the highest down. According to the evaluation:

- Faith was my number one gift from God. Well, I thought, how could I not have unusually high faith when I've actually been with God, and I know He's real?

- Hospitality was the gift from God that enabled me to love others and make them feel comfortable.
- Mercy was the gift of compassion. It showed I could understand stressful situations and encourage others with grace and dignity.
- Encouragement was my gift of the ability to lift another person and reassure them of the truth of having faith in God.
- Intercession was the fifth gift, which literally meant I would plead or pray on behalf of someone else. This said that I believed prayer worked and that I would pray for others.

When I arrived to the second Summit, everyone was casually chatting in the main foyer. The pastor's wife came over and introduced herself. "You look like someone who has a special message to give," she said.

I did have some messages—they were about my NDE and about how I saw angels on occasion in their church but I was quiet about them. The last time I'd shared my NDE at church, the lady had backed away in fear, telling me it was the work of the devil. I didn't want to subject myself to that kind of letdown again. Religious people were supposed to have unbending faith and an enduring belief in God, so I thought they'd be the first to be open to the truth that God was alive and well. That was not always the case. I'd only recently opened my heart to vulnerability again when I shared my experiences with Dr. Shelly, and while she believed me, I wasn't open to sharing with anyone else yet.

My initial response to the pastor's wife was, "No, no. I don't have any special messages." Little did I know at that moment that my silence was about to end. I was going to be shaken to my core and be forced to tell my story.

What I didn't know at that time was that God's Holy Spirit had had enough of my silence—He wanted to pull me out of my comfort zone. Before I tell you the rest of my story, I'll share with you a verse that gives good advice for God's people: "Trust the LORD with all your heart, and don't depend on your own understanding" (Proverbs 3:5 NCV).

I'll also remind you of what God said in Isaiah: "My thoughts are completely different from yours . . . my ways are far beyond anything you could imagine. For just as the heavens are higher than the earth, so are my ways higher than your ways and my thoughts higher than your thoughts" (Isaiah 55:8-9 NLT).

Three different Summit Meetings were being held that evening, and when the time came, I found mine and took a seat at the table. The room filled up, and as people mingled, a pleasant gentleman took a chair at my table and started asking others around us whether they had seen the movie *Heaven is for Real.*

Of course, the film was fresh in my mind, as were my other spiritual experiences, but since I had not yet heard from the pastor, I was reluctant to join the conversation. In fact, I got a little uptight, and my mind screamed: *Oh no, don't talk about that! I was hoping no one would talk about that!*

This kind man continued to inquire politely if anyone had seen the movie. He also expressed his personal thoughts, saying that he wasn't sure how true it was, because of how Colton—

in the film—had identified his great-grandfather who he saw in heaven. Colton had never met his great-grandfather because he had passed over before Colton was born. While in heaven, Colton met a man he called Pop, who he thought was very nice, who told him he used to play with Colton's dad. Colton eventually was able to identify Pop as a man in an old family picture, but not as portrayed in the movie. In real life, Colton identified the man named Pop in an old photograph in a more compelling fashion than the movie rendition. How that discovery was portrayed in the film made this gentleman question its validity.

In fact, after I saw the movie, still shaken by how my experiences connected to Colton's story and Kramarik's painting, I started reading the book, but I wasn't done with it yet. The book later depicted the real way Colton found the image of his great-grandfather, and it was more persuasive than how it had been depicted in the movie. I didn't respond to the man's comments immediately. I wasn't to that part in the book yet, but I knew the real story was slightly different than the film, since I'd read that on their website. I politely piped up and told him that I'd read on the website about the producers having made slight changes to the story that the family had agreed to for the purposes of the film. Then I sat quietly again.

The class began, and the teacher told us we'd be spending the evening talking about spiritual gifts. Her husband was assisting her with the session, and after the introductions, we discussed each kind of gift referred to in the test, and what each one meant. The leader said that none of us should worry about what was talked about while in this meeting, because this was a safe place to speak freely. She then asked the class, "Has anyone here had a spiritual experience?"

The group sat in silence.

"No one has had a spiritual experience?" The teacher waited for what seemed like forever—still no answer.

By that time, I was sweating from the nervousness and anxiety of not wanting to say anything. I sat with my head tilted down, rubbing my forehead, trying to be inconspicuous. The unease of my silence was mounting. I knew I should say something, but I didn't want to. To me, the silence was golden and kept me from experiencing the criticism of doubters. Inside my head, I was screaming, *OMG! Why did she ask that question?*

I hadn't expected this kind of conversation about the gifts God gave us, but there it was. God does everything in His own way. The question hung in the air, and she waited. And waited. And waited. The silence was deafening as everyone looked at each other, wondering if someone was going to share something interesting.

Time slowed. It was as if horns were sounding and little arrows hung in the air, like tiny, flashing neon signs pointing at me. I didn't really hear the sound or see the arrows, but I felt them.

Then God's Holy Spirit prodded me further. He wanted to be recognized. His prodding came to me not through my inner voice, but through my soul. The Holy Spirit started shaking me with the message—*acknowledge me!* The severity of this experience had never happened to this extent before, and it has not happened since.

My physical body sat in my chair trying to be invisible, when suddenly I felt my soul, that part of me that was my share of God's Holy Spirit, start to vibrate back and forth in my torso. It was as if that separate spirit body also sat in that chair, wiggling its own butt back and forth.

It's funny, but Gary Zukav's term the "Seat of the Soul" took on a new meaning for me that day. The seat of my soul was vibrating—fast and furiously. I felt, literally, like a human maraca; my soul shook its noisemaker loudly inside of me.

Despite the leader's earlier caveat that the meeting was a "safe place" for me, history had shown otherwise. But my spirit's maraca band was in full swing, and the intense vibrations inside me were overwhelming. So, I finally apprehensively asked the leader, "How safe is it here?"

"Very safe," she said.

I blurted out, "Well, then. I've died, and heaven is real because I've seen it. I was held in God's loving arms. I didn't want to say anything because I've called the church and the pastor hasn't called me back yet, and it's been three weeks." It was as if God or the Holy Ghost expelled those words from my mouth—I didn't have control over them.

Whoa! The looks on people's faces ranged from dumbfounded to disbelief. Mouths were agape and eyes widened. The leader exchanged glances with her husband. Time seemed to stop with certain astounded faces imprinted on my mind. Can you imagine the raised eyebrows and the stir I caused? The man who initially brought up *Heaven is for Real* said, "I never figured I'd know someone who'd had this kind of experience."

The leader of the group and her husband were kind and told me they'd find out why there had been such a delay as that was not normal. They were a service-oriented church, after all, and they felt there must have been a good reason behind the delay in the pastor having followed up with the guidance I had requested.

Then, the class resumed, or we took a break; I don't remember for sure. I just knew I couldn't believe the shake-up that had just happened.

When one of the pastors finally did call me back, he apologized for having taken so long. His assistant had been gone for a month, and he was behind in his duties. He read what I'd written about my experience in the letter I had sent, and said that these kinds of things do happen. He continued to add, however, that these types of experiences must not deviate from what is stated in the Bible. I replied that my experience didn't stray, and he agreed.

He responded that I should feel comfortable sharing my story. In fact, he encouraged me to share it, but said that I should make sure God got the credit.

What I learned was that it was more important to get God's approval rather than the approval of other people, because God was the one to get recognition from. The pastor specified that an NDE must not deviate from the Bible, and that proved to me that he was putting restrictions on what God could do. God was bigger and more omnipotent than any human's limitations.

It was interesting having recently found out while wrapping up the writing of this book that Dr. Mary Neal, Author of *To Heaven and Back: A Doctor's Extraordinary Account of Her*

Death, Heaven, Angels, and Life[23] had a similar message from God. Dr. Neal was directed to write a book and she too was procrastinating by letting life get in the way. She explains how one day it felt as if God had picked up her bed and threw her out of it, and told her it was time to write the book. She shares this experience while being interviewed on the internet show *Converging Zone.*[24]

It is also interesting to have discovered Pastor Benny Hinn of the Miracle Crusade had this same type of shaking experience as I had experienced during the Summit. His shake-up came when he was young. He wondered if it was the power of God and he was correct. He described this in his book *Good Morning Holy Spirit* when he was young and waiting for entrance into the meeting of a healing evangelist, Kathryn Kuhlman.[25]

Benny describes his body beginning to vibrate like someone had grabbed it and was shaking him. He noticed it started before entering the building and it didn't stop for three hours. He explains that evening that he was lost in spirit and sang the songs from his soul. He stated that he knew God had touched his life, but it was not like the way He touched him that evening. I have no doubt it was the Holy Spirit I was feeling, too.

It's also interesting to know Pastor Hinn had the same electric strikes I experienced after the car accident. In his book, he tells his readers how he felt millions of electric sensations like needles while he slept. Then he saw the Lord with his arms

---

[23] Neal, M. *To Heaven and Back.* New York: WaterBook Multnomah, 2012. E-book.
[24] "Dr. Mary Neal - Raised from the dead Part2 Converging Zone with Robert Ricciardelli." YouTube video, 30:51. Accessed June 20, 2014.
https://www.youtube.com/watch?v=ULsl92H-Noc
[25] Hinn, B. *Good Morning Holy Spirit.* Nashville: Thomas Nelson, Inc, 1997. E-book.

open wide.[26] I know the electrical feeling after my car accident was God's way of priming me for the ambush makeover that was coming. His ways are much higher than our ways and He's a very creative thinker!

The idea that some NDEr's stories are not considered real because they don't relate to similar details outlined in the Bible is akin to putting God in a box. The terminology any writer/experiencer uses to describe their NDE is personal to them, and God understands their thoughts. Each person's NDE is created to touch the spirit of the individual regardless of their belief systems and their own spiritual principles, but most importantly the reports of encountering a Light of pure love that is there for all of us is consistent despite of the method of arrival. This is not beyond the God I know!

As noted, in his book, *Life After Life*[27], Dr. Raymond Moody, who has studied the near-death experience since the early 1970s, found specific elements that were common. One of these elements was encountering The Supreme Being of Light that glows with all-encompassing love, compassion and kindness and the experiencer doesn't want to return to their earthly body. The Supreme Light appears as Jesus, an Ascended Master, or whatever belief system will touch the heart and spirit of that person.

God individualizes every NDE to suit the experiencer. He does not have to have human approval regarding what precisely He shows that individual.

---

[26] Hinn, B. *Good Morning Holy Spirit.* Nashville: Thomas Nelson, Inc, 1997. E-book.
[27] Moody, R. *Life After Life.* New York: HarperCollins Publishers, 2015.

13

JUDGMENT AND THE REVIEW PANEL

WHILE IN HEAVEN, OUR souls—our portion of God's Holy Spirit—live in pure love and bliss. Eventually, they decide they would like a new challenge. You could compare this, I suppose, to a person who loves to eat chocolate (I know I do!). But if I ate only chocolate, eventually I would long to eat something else. Granted, I could eat chocolate for a very long time, but in due course, potato chips or pizza would make my mouth water. It's as if our souls decide to eat chips instead of chocolate—rather than only receiving love, they choose to go on an earthly mission to express love.

While our souls are on their earthly missions, they also want to have the option to do other jobs for God, to advance to a higher level of helping God. For example, in the Bible, Paul described in 2 Corinthians 12:1-2 that he, Paul, was caught up to the third heaven. Paul's account was written like this: "This boasting is all so foolish but let me go on. Let me tell about the visions and revelations I received from the Lord. I was caught up into the third heaven fourteen years ago" (NLT).

When I was leaving heaven, I saw flashes of different beams of light, like an elevator quickly whizzing by the light of different floors or like watching an old-time movie spin on a reel as the empty frames flashed by in slow motion at the finish. These "frames," I knew, were dimensions. I cannot say for sure how many flashed by, but there were at least seven.

Wouldn't you, as a soul, want to work your way from the third to the highest dimension? Just like graduations from schools, one can only achieve higher levels by ascending to additional stages of learning. I know these life lessons are prearranged in the soul world under the supervision of more senior angelic beings, and the soul views their life adventure as an honor, not a task. I can say this without a doubt because I remember the enthusiasm and excitement I felt, as a soul, when returning to my body. I also know the planning panel in heaven shares in the joy and sense of accomplishment when the soul grasps the wisdom laid out for it to learn.

After my NDEs, I increasingly found myself in situations which seemed to be pre-arranged for my own spiritual advancement. It was as if I had agreed—in a meeting I did not consciously remember—to participate in soul-expanding events to develop my own spiritual being and intensify my spirit's longing for divine knowledge. Like wanting to change to potato chips or pizza after eating chocolate for a long time, my soul wanted to learn more lessons to add to its advancement.

One night, I found out the meaning of another vision I was shown during my third NDE when I was drawn up to heaven to engage in what I can only call a "Veiled Learning Program" on the topic of "Thou Shalt Not Judge."

In James 4:11-12, in a letter from a slave of God and Jesus, a slave named James wrote to Jewish Christians about not speaking evil against each other because we are not to judge. James states, "Don't speak evil against each other . . . God alone, who made the law, can rightly judge among us. He alone has the power to save or to destroy. So, what right do you have to condemn your neighbor?" (NLT).

On this night, I'd fallen into bed after a great day. As usual, I read for a while, and when my eyes grew heavy, I fell into restful sleep. I remember being drawn back up to the celestial white space in heaven. This was the same dimension of heavenly whiteness where I'd seen Doug shortly after his funeral, and the same ethereal space my spirit had been in when I'd heard the lady's voice say "namaste."

This time, however, I found myself standing before a panel of angelic beings—the same panel of spiritual beings I was shown in a vision during my third NDE. Some were sitting at a table and some stood. They were dressed in white robes, and I knew, somehow, that we were already familiar with each other. I also knew that they were the same panel who had planned how my life would be orchestrated for me to learn. I, on the other hand, did not consciously remember being involved in this planning process. I may have given myself the lessons I wanted to learn, but at this point, I only knew that I was the student. I drew a picture of the committee after I returned from the experience, shown below.

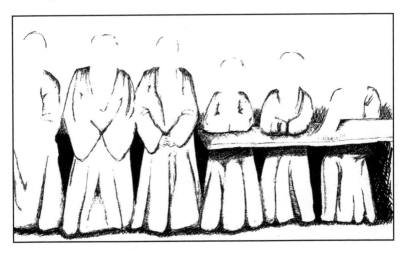

Figure 13 The panel of spiritual beings who were present for the "Thou Shalt Not Judge" lesson review.

On this occasion, the committee wanted to know if I'd learned anything about the so-called eleventh commandment, "Thou Shalt Not Judge." Of course, they already knew I had. I told them proudly, "Yes, I have!" and they asked me to share with them what I'd learned and how I'd learned it.

As I explained, a holographic movie showing them my memories played across the sky. The motion picture consisted of the remembered events that had caused me to form a judgment. Then, I showed them everything that had happened that made me realize I'd come to the wrong conclusion. I knew I'd misjudged, and I told them that. I learned my lesson.

The panel of beings was pleased about how I'd progressed. I was impressed with them, too, because they knew precisely what I, as a soul, had wanted to learn in this lifetime. They knew that the events I'd been shown were some of the reasons my soul chose this experience—everything had been laid out for my soul to learn.

"But why can't we know what our lessons are in life?" you might ask. Because our learning can't happen if we as a soul retain that planned knowledge when we enter our earthly body, so the knowledge is veiled and revealed over time through life experience.

I continued to share my lessons about how I had learned about judgment with the panel. Some of the stories seemed mundane, but not all of our experiences need to be earth-shattering for us to adequately learn them. Looking back on these lessons, they seemed so well-defined that they unfolded precisely as they needed to in my life in order for me to truly embrace the learning.

While growing up, I believed that we should all be modest and keep our bodies well-covered. I can't say I was taught this; rather, it was a conclusion I came to on my own. When I was little, I usually wore pants to play in, but occasionally I wore a dress, especially when going to church. I loved those frilly clothes, and for short periods of time, I acted like the little lady I was supposed to be. That was, of course, until I saw a group of children playing and wanted to join them.

It was during those times, I was told to either keep my dress down or go change my clothes. Maybe it was something as innocent and straightforward as that admonition that caused me to form my strict opinion about dignity and decorum. Suffice it to say that I perceived that discretion and modesty ought to be the norm.

I had a best friend whose dad was an outstanding member of the community and well-respected by everyone who knew him, but his choice of an athletic bathing suit during the hot and humid summers was, shall we say, unusual to me. He was a good, kind man who loved his family, and he worked hard. He built a massive swing set and slide for his children and the neighborhood kids to play on. He loved to garden and care for his flowers, and he enjoyed selling apples from the orchard in his backyard.

He bought a ten-foot-wide cattle-watering tank and filled it for us children to swim in, to escape the hot and humid Midwest summers. During those blistering days, he also tried to keep cool by wearing a briefs-type swimsuit similar to what Olympic swimmers wear. This swimsuit bothered me because of its limited coverage.

We didn't have television when I was very young, and when we did get one, we only had two and eventually three channels. At that time, there was no Olympic games coverage or even much sports coverage, so swimming attire for men was not in my sphere of experience. Today, the briefs-type swimsuit is standard attire for Olympic swimming events—and under modern-day circumstances, the suits look perfectly reasonable to me.

But back in those days, I was unaccustomed to being around people who were comfortable wearing minimal, tight-fitting clothing. As silly as it sounds, from as far back as childhood, I formed a dislike for the look of men's brief swimsuits. I made a strong judgment about it, and I carried that judgment into adulthood.

How did the spiritual panel orchestrate my lesson of "Thou Shalt Not Judge"? They had me meet and fall in love with a man named Bob. Bob was from Austria, and he loved to swim in the many lakes where he lived. This was yet another example of the panel's clever planning. I couldn't have learned how wrong I'd judged my friend's dad if God and his committee hadn't worked out the details of me meeting Bob.

When Bob came to visit me in America, he inquired about swimming because from the plane, he'd seen all the lakes that dotted our terrain. Unfortunately, the lakes along the foothills of the Rocky Mountains were filled with cold mountain water, so they were unfriendly by his standards. The lakes in the country he came from are much warmer and cleaner.

Bob was also surprised to see the style of swimsuit typical in the United States at that time. Men's swimsuits looked like regular shorts down to the knees. In his younger days, Bob had trained for swimming and diving with an Olympic coach, so he was astonished—he couldn't understand why men swam with so much wet clothing dragging around their waists. Men in Europe usually wear the well-known briefs-type swimsuits.

When he told me about his type of swimsuit, all of those memories from childhood came flooding back. What were the chances I would meet someone who wore that type of swimwear, when every other male I'd known wore swim trunks down to their knees? Bob explained to me that Olympic swimmers wear the briefs-type suit because there was less drag in the water. I understood that concept, but still, I had a cultural adjustment to make.

The European lifestyle was also an adjustment for me because they were a free people, compared to the way I was brought up. For example, it was common for sunbathers on beaches to take off their swimsuits in public and change into their dry clothing without anyone making a fuss. To them, a body was a body, and everyone has one. They didn't march around without clothing on, but changing out of a wet swimsuit to dry wear on the beach was acceptable.

Many spas in Europe have saunas where clothes are forbidden because swimsuits are seen as harboring bacteria, but people were at least provided with a towel. Oh, and lest I forget, their saunas are often times unisex. All of these things told me that Europeans had a higher level of comfort with their bodies than we had in the United States. The no-clothing-in-the-sauna rule was a health issue for them; they considered it unsanitary due to the bacteria clothing could harbor. Did that make either of us wrong? Not at all. There are cultural differences we must be aware of when visiting other lands, especially with world travel as easy as it is these days.

Everything I'd learned from Bob about Europe made me think about my girlfriend's dad, and how similar his ways were to the Europeans'. My friend's family even had friends from Europe who came to visit them. I remember this because the children of this couple taught us to count to ten in Hungarian.

Putting all of this together, I realized that America was a land of immigrants with many kinds of lifestyles. My neighbor's choice of swimming attire seemed reasonable to him, even though it may not have been the style I was accustomed to. Upon reflection, if he'd worn knee-length shorts, I wouldn't have thought anything about it because I was used to that style. I'd made a judgment without knowing all the facts.

This concept of non-judgment is referred to in Paul's letters to Corinth. Paul's letters describe what he learned during his time in heaven, and I can confirm his lessons from my own spiritual experiences, as well. Paul writes that "no one can know what anyone else is really thinking except that person alone, and no one can know God's thoughts except God's own Spirit" (1 Corinthians 2:11 NLT).

This is true. How can we see another person's complete story or understand their emotional views regarding things that have happened in their lives unless we are that person? How can we possibly relate to the depth of someone's thoughts and how their feelings have developed over their lifetime?

I also told the panel that I realized that I may have judged my grandfather unjustly too, due to listening and believing the views of someone else.

My grandfather came to America from Norway as a little boy. I wondered if Norwegian people were very social, too. Did they share friendship over a beer or a glass of wine like many other European countries? My grandfather was said to have a drinking problem, but I began to wonder: if he'd genuinely had a drinking problem, how could he have suddenly become a bartender and quit drinking?

The time frame of my grandfather's so-called drinking problem seemed to have been when his marriage was falling apart. I was told his marriage failed because my grandmother had fallen in love with our "extra grandfather," Elmer.

It may have been the other way around, though. Did my grandmother seek the love she was looking for in the arms of another man because her husband spent so much time in the bars? Or was there more to the picture?

My grandfather served in World War II and was honorably discharged. Like so many other men of his time, I'm sure he spent a lot of time in Europe. Movies seem to depict military personnel as often taking leave at a local bar if they were in a safe environment. While in the army, had my grandfather become accustomed to sharing comradery over drinks? Did he have a post-traumatic stress disorder from his war experience? Was he trying to drown his problems?

I accepted that the stories of my grandfather's drinking problem were true. In essence, I judged him to be the-person-with-the-alcohol-problem when everything I'd seen and experienced of my grandfather was not that man. The grandfather I saw never had a drink in his hand. He was always kind and he loved his grandchildren.

As a child, I lived in a house where I could run out back and play in the woods, smell flowers along the dirt road, and dig up wild turnips and dust them off to eat. I climbed trees and pretended they were spaceships. Sitting in the crotch of two branches that became my Captain's Chair, I navigated, in my imagination, this tree-ship into the wild blue yonder.

While we lived in a suburb of the city, my grandfather rented an apartment above a furniture store in the downtown area. *Why would anyone want to live in an apartment above a shop?* I wondered. It wasn't normal, and I couldn't fathom it. I thought he was too financially destitute to live otherwise, so I'd also judged my grandfather's living conditions.

Now that I've been to Europe, I've seen the many tall buildings that accommodate stores on the main floor and apartments on the levels above. This is typical of the apartment homes many families live in, and I now know that this kind of accommodation is lovely, warm, comfortable, and delightful—and convenient to city transportation systems.

My grandfather came from the European way of life, having spent some of his childhood in Norway. So, apartment living may have been a comfortable way of life for him. Who was I to have made these kinds of judgments?

In those days, there were no malls, so all his entertainment was downtown. Movie theaters and shops were located downtown too. City bus transportation was active when my grandfather lived downtown and his lifestyle when I was a child was reminiscent of what I see in Europe today. So, once again, I finally saw that I'd made a judgment that his way of life was not quite right because it wasn't the way I was living.

I also learned through having met Bob that countries throughout Europe have beautiful vineyards. The beer and wine industries are prominent, and people love to come together and socialize. There are beer festivals with traditional music and dance, and miles of pathways weave through vineyard after vineyard, with little stops along the way where you can share a glass of wine with other travelers.

The little stops throughout the vineyards reminded me of a charming tradition Europeans have during the winter holiday season. In many cities throughout Europe, during the Christmas season huts are set up throughout the city, colorfully decorated with twinkling lights where you can buy a concoction they call Punsch, a hot wine, rum, and fruit mixture that reminds me of the hot apple cider with a cinnamon stick we Americans drink during the festive season. The areas around these huts are heated, and one can stand at high tables visiting with other guests who have also stopped to imbibe.

Even though my grandfather was young when he came to America, did he remember his family's lifestyle in Europe? Did he watch adults sharing a drink in this fashion? Was he emulating them? Was this how my grandfather was raised? Was drinking merely his fun way of socializing? Had my grandfather been unfairly judged by everyone?

No one can know another person's entire story, or know what has made them the person they are. I'm a prime example of that fact—no one knows my full story. This will be the first time that many of my family, even those closest to me, will hear the details of my life. These personal experiences and thoughts have created the person I am today.

Even though the world is enormous, it gets smaller every year as international travel becomes faster. Cultural differences collide in many parts of our world, so compassion and understanding of cultural norms are required in today's societies. Keep an open mind and realize that your ways may be as strange to someone else as their customs are to you.

We must remember the Golden Rule that Jesus gave us during the most well-known sermon of all time: the Sermon on the Mount. Jesus says, "Do for others what you would like them to do for you. This is a summary of all that is taught in the law and the prophets" (Matthew 7:12 NLT).

The review on "Thou Shalt Not Judge" came to an end. The spiritual beings who were a part of God's staff were pleased and joyful with what I'd learned. The panelists nodded their heads, murmuring delightfully to each other, and we all were amused and chuckling.

It was time for me to go. I distinctly remember saying to the panel, "That was so cleverly laid out for me to learn." I remember shaking my head in amazement and laughing as I was sent back to my physical body. I even woke up with a smile on my face, still shaking my head and chuckling because what had happened was so thought-provoking and exciting.

It was interesting to know this lesson was not only for me, but for Bob, too. Bob held a very prominent, investigative position and was skeptical about my story, but the "revved-up energy" that initiates electrical malfunctions around me still happens today, especially when I meet with another NDEr. Recently, within several months, I interviewed two other NDErs as part of my studies of spiritual experiences, with the intention of including these interviews in a book.

One evening after an interview, while I was cooking dinner, the kitchen light blew out—not a big deal in the scheme of things.

Then, the television came on by itself. When that happened, Bob looked at me. We had discussed the electrical snafus that happened to me, but Bob was, like I said, still a skeptic.

In this instance, he dismissed the snapping lightbulb, but the combination of the light bulb and the television popping on by itself was not so easy to discount. Earlier he had accompanied me to an interview, and after the interview, we found that my cell phone no longer worked. The circuits were so fried I couldn't even retrieve my contact information and, on that same evening, the kitchen light—instead of turning off by itself—turned on.

At the time the phone died, Bob sloughed it off saying it was an old phone, but again after another interview and more electrical problems followed, it was getting harder for him to discount. I smiled and said, "See, I told you." Bob now thinks that NDEs and all that occurs around them are fascinating.

Bob also now thinks the electrical phenomena is not so amusing because it seems to cause my computer to fail. As I write this, Bob has had to rebuild my crashed computer three times since the purchase four years ago. Why did I purchase a new computer back then? Because, just like the cell phone, my old computer crashed so badly I lost everything and had to start over again.

Jesus doesn't want us to condemn others, or to judge them. For example, if we speak poorly of someone who is gossiping, and then we go to a friend's house and gossip, we are a hypocrite. Before we can help clean up someone else's house, so to speak, we need to clean up our own. Jesus speaks of this on the Sermon on the Mount:

"Stop judging others, and you will not be judged. For others will treat you as you treat them. Whatever measure you use in judging others, it will be used to measure how you are judged. And why worry about a speck in your friend's eye when you have a log in your own? How can you think of saying, 'Let me help you get rid of that speck in your eye,' when you can't see past the log in your own eye? Hypocrite! First get rid of the log from your own eye; then perhaps you will see well enough to deal with the speck in your friend's eye." (Matthew 7:1-5 NLT)

14
PROPOSED PATHS, GUIDANCE, AND CHOICES

WHEN I SHARED THE story of my allergy-induced NDE, I described how my awareness melded with God's consciousness. Remember when I mentioned that in 2 Corinthians 12:4, Paul said that he heard things so astounding they couldn't be told? I believe that the "astounding things" that Paul could not share might include the knowledge that events in our lives are predetermined, that we live many lifetimes, that heavenly helpers exist, and that heaven is a place of many increasingly sophisticated levels of consciousness so we, as souls, are here to learn.

Can you imagine how that information might have been received had Paul shared it in the first century AD? He had a devil of a time (pun intended) sharing the messages he did.

Thankfully, our modern societies are more advanced and more tolerant, so it's time that more of these truths be shared.

In light of all of this, you might ask, "Why do we want to learn?" We all are here because on the soul level, we choose to be here. We are honored and excited to take on the challenge of being of service to this individual. We come to this little blue planet to live, learn, and evolve. Just think of all the people around you as other souls having human experiences. Our souls are working in tandem with our physical bodies, as God's insiders or undercover agents, so to speak.

We are God's advocates, living in a physical body, communicating to the individual we are guiding. We use the method of thought implant (that's the simplest way to explain it), giving emotional or physical sensations, such as the gut instinct or a sense of unease, to gently nudge the individual in one direction versus another, always directing them toward the best route in their life.

After my consciousness connection with the Divine and His voice guiding me to understand the visionary moments He flashed before me, I set out on a quest to learn. I recognized some of the significant ways that God's Holy Spirit has guided me through life. I've shared most of these instances with you in this book, and each time I came to a conclusion as to the reason behind these miraculous occurrences, Jesus made His presence known with a message that I was correct.

I have no doubt that all of what I shared with you is what I see to be the truth. I'll remind you about our life's navigational system that is referred to in Psalm 32:8: "The LORD says, 'I will guide you along the best pathway for your life. I'll advise you and watch over you'" (NLT). This verse plainly says the best path for us it's not the only pathway.

Often, we'll hear our inner voice nagging at us when we need to choose one thing versus another. It is not only the big choices our guides help us with—whether to move, or marry, or take a certain job. It is also the small choices. Should we buy that new pair of shoes? Should we eat that candy bar? Even something so little as the thought, *you're going to tip that over,* when you set your drink down. Sometimes, if the "still, small voice" within us says no to something we want, we may disregard it as being merely an irritating influence—we don't listen.

We buy those pretty new shoes that prove to be uncomfortable, or we happily devour the delicious candy bar that leaves us feeling guilty, or after disregarding that inner warning, we knock that drink over and now have a mess. Those are the times when we are exercising the free will that God has given us. I'll give you a few examples from my own life about how we, on the soul level, know our path and the events that will unfold in our lives.

One question many of us often ask is, "If God is watching over us, why do bad things happen in our lives?" Yes, cruel things do happen; however, that's why God said He will guide us along the best path. It is essential for us to know that there are two orders at work within the human body: one is the guidance system of spirit, or the proverbial good angel sitting on one shoulder, and the other is ego, who rests on the other shoulder.

The ego, as I mentioned earlier, is that side that gets in the way and "edges God out" (which is why it's called the E.G.O.).

It's not that terrible things are preordained; it's more akin to the perpetrators having failed their lessons and gone astray. Sometimes we, as souls, choose difficult lessons so we can advance faster when we grasp the learning.

Our choice—and there's always a choice determines what path we take and what lessons we learn. God didn't promise us a comfortable life with no problems. If life was trouble-free, if there weren't hazards along the way, if there was always light and no darkness, how would we learn our lessons? What would we compare them to? When we encounter rough times, it is advantageous to look at what each of our experiences is teaching us.

If we learn how to listen to our inner guidance, our lives can be drastically changed. We can look back on our lives and see examples of choices we made that we may regret—or we can realize that if we had made a different decision, we would have been set upon a different life path. The following examples from my own life that are particularly poignant. The first one happened when I was five or six years old.

IN THOSE DAYS, LIFE was straightforward. We didn't have the crime we see today in society. Our mom knew most of the neighbors, we knew the other children our age, and all our parents watched out for the neighborhood children. We were taught to be wary of strangers, but ours was a safe community—at least we thought it was.

One evening at dinnertime, my brothers were late coming home from playing. My mom asked me to go outside, find the boys, and tell them to come in for dinner. "But don't go too far," she said. I looked in all the usual places, including our neighbor's gigantic swing set, and they weren't there. I looked down the street in one direction and up the street in the other direction, but still, I didn't see them.

We lived next door to a charming married couple who didn't have children, and on the other side of their house was a vacant lot. Next to them was another home. The man who lived there was on the porch. Since I didn't know him, and I was wary of getting too close, I walked across the charming couple's front yard and stopped at the edge of the vacant lot.

From across the empty lot, I asked, "Are my brothers in your house?"

I wasn't sure my brothers knew his kids, but I was pretty smart and knew that you never get anywhere if you don't ask.

The neighbor answered, "No, but would you like to come in? You could see for yourself."

I heard a little voice in my left ear say distinctly, "Leave."

I felt uncomfortable, and I followed that guidance, telling him no. I turned and walked—then ran—all the way home.

I never said anything to my mom about the neighbor because I let it go. Much later, though, I discovered that the unease I felt and the voice I'd heard was divine guidance—it had protected me. We found out years later that particular neighbor was a child molester. What might have happened if I'd ignored the voice and gone into his house?

We should consider as well that on a soul level, we may have agreed to participate in situations in which other souls can learn their lessons—just as other souls may have decided to participate in ours. For example, remember when my daughter Gina came to me during my first NDE? Perhaps I had made a soul contract with her to be her mom, but if I'd died, she wouldn't have been born fifteen years later.

Had she come to remind me of our contract and I chose to stay and honor that agreement? I give you a resounding, "Yes!" Likewise, I'd plainly made a soul contract to help my son Curt. I was there with him at the right time, and my influence started him on the path to a new and better life. Again, this supports the planning of life paths and events.

This leaves my oldest son, Phillip, who has been the rock in our family. Did we have a soul contract? I believe we did, and though he didn't appear in any of my NDE visions, he has helped each of us in some way.

Phillip moved in with me after Curt got married and moved out. If Phillip had not done this, I would have had to relocate before I was ready. When the recession hit, Gina found herself unemployed for over a year. Phillip stepped in, rented her home, and moved in until she was established in a new job. Years later, when Curt went through a divorce, Phillip opened his arms and his home to Curt and his daughter.

I am confident that Phillip's soul loved the rest of us profoundly, and generously offered to come and stabilize the boat during challenging times. We all sail together across life's stormy seas, but as the sailors on a ship, it takes teamwork to make a successful passage.

Needless to say, there are some pretty challenging lives that some souls volunteer to live, but the Holy Spirit loves us all unconditionally and will never give up on the lesson plan that was laid out for each of us. We must always realize God's promises are true, His plans are to lead us to our best life, and He is always there to help and love us. We may veer off course due to choices we've made, but God's Holy Spirit persistently tries to get us back on the path that is best for us.

NOW, LET'S GET BACK to the question: "Why learn?" Recall once again that in the Bible, Paul describes that he was caught up in the third heaven.

Our souls inhabit human bodies to experience life on the earthly plane. I believe that our souls "sign up" to live through predetermined events so that we can learn lessons and thereby raise our levels of consciousness. Of course, here in the earthly realm, we all have free will, and we can opt out of any preordained events should we choose. But by and large, before we were born, we committed to earthly life to learn, grow, and elevate our soul-selves to a higher plane.

An example of a lesson plan is in the chapter about the review panel. I shared a story about Bob, whom I remembered from another life. I saw him in a vision before we met in this lifetime. I didn't initially realize the man in the vision was Bob because it took his physical aging to reveal the undeniable likeness.

I wouldn't have learned how I had misjudged my best friend's dad or my grandfather in the way I had if Bob hadn't come into my life. Without Bob, I wouldn't have gone to a part of the world where I could see and learn how I had misjudged. Just think of the coordination it took for God to have guided Bob to come to know me from almost the other side of the globe.

I have come to understand most of what God revealed during my third NDE, but it was a learning process. God guides us through life, giving us a host of support and advisers for our life journeys, among them Jesus, the Holy Spirit, angels, and a myriad of others. I know this is true because this knowledge is part of the higher awareness He bestowed me. And as you know, I've seen the otherworldly entities that are here to help us.

If we are open, if we listen, the spirit will protect and guide us. Sometimes, the soul will share great wisdom with us that can help us navigate our life's plan. Occasionally, divine wisdom will come to us in packets of insight. Other times, it happens in broad, visionary strokes, which I call "downloads."

After my third NDE, I was still blind to precisely what these downloads of information meant. It takes time—sometimes years—to understand how we can use this downloaded knowledge to our best advantage. Why? Because sometimes, the confusion we feel can keep us from perceiving the benefits and gifts that an NDE brings. The mere practicality of staying alive can override any spiritual revelations that might be buried in the experience.

In my case, for example, I knew I'd almost died, and I wasn't ready to go. After my third NDE, I hadn't thought about looking into the spiritual meaning of the experience—I didn't know there was a name for what happened and I didn't know where to even start to gather information. I was living my life again, trying to put the unexplainable behind me like I did after the other NDEs. But Jesus continued knocking at my door and wanted me to clearly understand the wisdom He bestowed on me. He kicked His ingenious talents of orchestration into gear!

How did Jesus orchestrate this? He guided me to a book that brought clarity. I eventually came to understand the complexity and depth of what had happened to me. I needed a nudge, and He gave me one.

NEARLY TWO YEARS AFTER my big NDE, Gina called asking for help. She had had a terrible recurring dream and wanted to know if I could help her find out what it meant. I didn't know anything about dream interpretation, but when your child asks for help, you help. I told her to come up for the weekend and we'd go to the bookstore. I knew there were books written on dream interpretation, and that seemed like a logical start.

Gina drove up to the ranch from college on a Friday evening. On Saturday, we set out for the bookstore, filled with anticipation. We both loved bookstores; there was always something of interest—love stories, games, calendars—and I especially relish romance stories.

We browsed and flipped through various dream interpretation books—amazingly, there was a lot. Many suggested that ordinary items seen in a dream have symbolic significance. I didn't feel comfortable interpreting the symbolism in Gina's dream, so I kept looking. Suddenly, my eyes were drawn to a book. It was as if the book pulled me to it like a magnet. It had a simple, dark blue cover, with large, easy-to-read print. I immediately knew this was the book we needed. It was called *Book of Dreams*[28], written by the late Sylvia Browne. Gina was busy with her studies and a part-time job, so I told her I would read the book and give her a recap.

It was fun having mom and daughter time later that day, and we couldn't resist glancing through our new purchase and reading tidbits of interest. I was anxious to dive into the book, so after Gina drove back to college and the ranch chores were done, I settled into my comfy recliner with a cold refreshment and the book. It was absorbing, enlightening, and captured my attention—I read it day after day in my spare time. When I found something interesting and pertinent to Gina's predicament, I grabbed the phone, read a few passages to her, and we discussed it.

At the end of the book, Sylvia Browne had inserted an excerpt of another one of her books, *Visits from the Afterlife*[29]. The bells and whistles started blaring in my head—imaginary confetti were falling everywhere! Browne, in that sample, described specific features of our trip to heaven after the body dies. Suddenly, I had clarity for what had happened to me two years earlier. I'd suffocated to death on that night and had been on my way to heaven!

Sylvia Browne explains the experience of death as including being out-of-body, feeling weightless freedom, feeling negativity

---

[28] Browne, S., & Harrison, L. *Book of Dreams.* New York: New American Library, 2003.
[29] Browne, S., & Harrison, L. *Visits from the Afterlife.* New York: New American Library, 2003. E-book.

melting away, and being replaced with the feeling of love and peace, as well as seeing a brilliant tunnel of light and the all-loving Light of God.[30] She describes exactly what had happened to me on the night when I couldn't breathe. I knew that God had guided me to this book so that Gina and I could both have the answers that we'd been seeking.

Sylvia Browne's book was pivotal in both my life and Gina's lives. Browne's story helped Gina discover what she needed to do in her personal life to resolve her nightmare, and I learned what happened to me in my NDEs. That knowledge gave me a sense of peace and set me on a course of discovery that ultimately provided me with a profound, broad understanding of the miraculous experiences I'd had. My insecurities about everything that was happening to me now made sense, and I began to incorporate my recently discovered knowledge into my life to create a new and exciting future. I accepted my new reality and began to heal.

Everyone in our modern world is searching for clarity on life's challenges, not just NDErs. In troubling and confusing times, we ask questions like, "What happened? Why did it happen? What did I do wrong? What does it mean?" We want answers to our own, specific questions, and even if the answers we get are not what we want to hear, having a way out helps us deal with our dilemmas. Truth helps bring resolution and frees us from what's troubling us so we can start creating a better future.

I know that Jesus directed Gina and I to the bookstore that day. He used Gina's nightmare to inspire her to call me, and that

[30] Browne, S., & Harrison, L. *Book of Dreams,* pp. 276-277. New York: New American Library, 2003.

call set up a chain reaction of events. Jesus guided us to the bookstore and made that book draw me in like metal to a magnet.

That book taught me not only about my death experience, but led me to Sylvia Browne's other books about angels and about how they are always around us, wanting to help. That chain of events guided me to a course of learning I needed at that time in my life. I have no doubt at this point in my life that I would not know the scope and depth of these spiritual experiences had I made a choice to give up on helping my daughter.

What is the bottom line? The I AM—that all-encompassing, divine entity that we call God—was personally involved in all that has happened to me on this astonishing journey. Jesus guided me, and He didn't leave me to flounder. He knew I needed to understand, and He wanted me to realize the profound wisdom of the gift that was given to me. He gave me direction and set me on a path to search for answers. Today, He continues to guide me to the places and people I need to connect with.

Another important point is we are not victims of life. We may be victims of certain horrible circumstances, but we shouldn't let those situations steal the rest of our life. Heaven wants us to experience joy and all the happy emotions we possibly can. Considering our consciousness is a slice of the Super Creator, we are all the creators, or architects, if you will, of our own reality. By clearing away the negative or stressful debris of energy around us and replacing it with beautiful flowers and tranquil waterfalls, we can create a more positive environment for the life we choose. Our choices, our optimistic thoughts, and our intentions to move forward in life can fill our life with peace, beauty, joy, love, and happiness. If we live with gratitude and positivity, and trust in God, we can change the way we experience life.

One example of a prearranged life was when my parents started their family, living in a small, two-bedroom bungalow. Back in those days, there were no sonogram machines, so when their first baby boy came into this world and the doctor announced there was another baby on the way, everyone was surprised and delighted. As was the tradition in those days, my dad passed out many cigars in celebration of the arrival of Dennis and Douglas.

I followed two years later. Once I arrived, our family needed more substantial accommodation, so my parents decided to build a new house. After the stud walls had been put in place and the rooms were identifiable, my dad wanted to show my mom the progress in person. He loaded us all into the car and off we drove to see our future home.

We all remember the first memory in our lives, and my first memory is of the day my dad showed us our new home. I was maybe one and a half to two years old. I couldn't yet walk well on my own, and my mom held me in the crux of her left arm. My dad was excited to show my mom the layout of the kitchen. He showed her where the cupboards were going, and, standing in front of the imagined island of lower cabinets, he said animatedly, "Here's where the sink will go." Then he showed her where the stove and refrigerator would be. I watched him as he spoke excitedly and used his hands to describe our new kitchen—the heart of our family's home.

I can remember that day as if it's happening now: there was a breeze blowing through the house and strands of my mom's brown hair blew across my face. It was a chilly day, cloudy and overcast. It was not quite spring, because everything still looked wintery. The grass was brown and there were no leaves on the trees.

It's strange that I remember this event so vividly even though I was so small. I understood everything my dad was describing and could picture it in my mind exactly as it was going to be when completed. This was truly amazing, especially when you keep in mind that the average vocabulary for a child at that age is 140-300 words. At eighteen months, children start to connect words such as "car go" or "my ball" or "Daddy go."[31]

How did I—a toddler in my mom's arms—understand everything that was being said that day? I knew precisely what the kitchen of our future home was going to look like. How could I have known this unless it was already arranged before I came into this life?

I felt as though I was watching my dad through two portholes, through the two eyes of this baby girl. Can you imagine looking out over your life's events from the glass hole of an airplane or a ship? I know that sounds awfully strange, but I believe that my soul was viewing everything that day, through the eyes of the child that was me. That soul was my gift from God, my piece of the Holy Spirit, my guide and counselor. This, my first memory, was the first point in my life that proved to me that our paths and options are orchestrated before we are born.

---

[31] "Child Development Tracker, Language." *PBS*. Accessed November 7, 2017. http://www.pbs.org/parents/childdevelopmenttracker/one/language.html

My "porthole" point of view was a straightforward example of how our spirit sees through the eyes of the person they are guiding. I can easily say this, since I have witnessed firsthand that we are spiritual beings having a human experience. As Paul writes:

> "Our dying bodies make us groan and sigh, but it's not that we want to die and have no bodies at all. We want to slip into our new bodies so that these dying bodies will be swallowed up by everlasting life. God himself has prepared us for this, and as a guarantee, he has given us his Holy Spirit." (2 Corinthians 5:4-5 NLT)

This verse refers to the soul as God's Holy Spirit entering a body when it comes to this world to help. Once the body starts dying, the soul slips back into its spiritual body form when it returns to heaven.

It is your soul energy that is reading this book through the eyes of your physical body. Your soul lives its life to learn its lessons, then separates from the body at the time predestined in the Book of Life. This is why when the soul, our life force, leaves the body, the body ceases to function. Sometimes, however, through accidents or illness, we might be given the opportunity to pass over early. If it's not our scheduled time, then we might be given a choice—through a near-death experience, for example—to go back to our physical body or to pass over into the spirit world.

In my view, NDEs are not only opportunities for a soul to recalibrate its life path, but in some instances, like mine, NDEs are prearranged so the NDEr can share the truths that God has given to him or her. Why do I believe this? Because in the case of an NDE, if it had been the scheduled date of departure, the soul would have just zipped over to the spirit world in the blink of an eye. And once the soul does decide to leave this mortal world, the soul and our consciousness, with all its current life memories, continue to live on in the eternal world of bliss. But that is not the only reason.

I also believe this because of the information and flashes of past and future events of my life. Some of these instances include my predicted death at pre-kindergarten age, the music box lady, the car accident, the ambush makeover, the crowd of people where I prayed for healing, the image of Curt, the panel of angelic beings, and the oil rig that ended up giving me a nice income, after I'd realized that material things don't make happiness. Virtually every event I've shared in this book was an image I saw.

How do you know what your life lessons are? How do you know if you've learned the lessons your soul set out for you before you came to the physical realm? There's an easy way to find out: create your own Book of Life. Make a timeline, as I did. You might want to choose a beautiful journal for this exercise, and find some quiet time when you can be alone and contemplate the life you've led so far.

First, record all the prominent events in your life, including moments of déjà vu. These are instances when you've felt like you've been here before or you've done this before. These moments may correlate with those important memories you've recorded in your journal, and they can lead you to remember (or to just know, in your heart) that you were on the path planned for you.

After you contemplate your life's journey for a while, ask yourself:

- Did these events lead me in a direction that was beneficial to me?
- What did I learn from these experiences? Was it empathy, compassion, love, kindness, or patience?
- Was I following the Golden Rule to love others as I loved myself?
- Do I see a pattern in my own behavior that I need to overcome?
- Before you comment upon or act upon something that is said or that happened, ask yourself: Is this response the way I want to show my love?
- Did I not get what I wanted because I was wishing for it to happen instead of acting on it? Was I putting up my own roadblocks? If so, try changing your personal power affirmation from "can I?" or "I can't" to the powerful, manifesting thought, "I can!"
- Are the people I surround myself with lifting me up and inspiring me to be the best I can be?
- After reviewing the Book of Life you have created, would it be beneficial to you or someone else to clarify a misunderstood situation?

Having done this exercise myself, I have gone back and tied up loose ends with my relationships. That's how serious I am about learning my life's lessons. Perhaps there are things in your life that need to be cleared up—are there wounds, rifts, or misunderstandings that need to be solved or healed? Can you resolve them? The important point is to be *aware* of how you have affected other people's lives and to decide how you can best live in God's way for the rest of your life.

Now that I've learned to accept the divine guidance I'm given, I view my life as an adventure rather than a challenge. I think it's going to be a hoot to see how well I did in deciphering my own Book of Life when I get to heaven! Even though I'm nearly done writing this book God told me to write, I still cannot say that I'm all I should be in his eyes. Like you, I'm human, and ego keeps getting in my way.

I'm eternally thankful for every difficult person and every difficult moment for having made me the person I am today. Each of those lessons were important to my soul's advancement, and I'm astounded at all that I've learned. Now, I am focusing all of my energy on being the most I can be and helping—or at least understanding—the people He puts in my path. Life is a fun adventure, and I look forward to seeing where He leads me next.

15

THE FUNDAMENTAL TRUTHS OF HEAVEN AND THE NATURE OF THE SOUL

WHAT MAKES SOMETHING RELIABLE? When you get in your car every morning, and it starts without a problem, you know your car is reliable. When you want to check your weight, and your scale gives you your correct weight, then you know the scale is reliable. When someone always shows up on time and does what they say they're going to do, you know they are reliable.

When you get the same results or the same answer repeatedly, you know that the information you are getting, or the equipment you are using, is reliable. When it comes to near-death and other types of spiritually transformative experiences, increasingly more people are reporting having had similar experiences, so we know their information is reliable.

The NDERF, the Near-Death Experience Research Foundation, shares statistics it has gathered from various sources.[32]

The results of a study on NDEs done in Germany, for example, found that four percent of the German population have had an NDE, while according to a Gallup Poll in 1982[33], five percent of the people in the United States have had one in their lives. NDERF's conclusion for the United States was 774 NDEs occur daily. That's 282,510 NDEs per year!

Writer, researcher, and NDE-experiencer P.M.H. Atwater has studied NDE traits, phenomena, and aftereffects for over thirty years. In her book *Near-Death Experiences; The Rest of the Story*,[34] she shares her NDE studies, which were based on her observations and the cross-checking of 3,000 adults and 277 child experiencers.

Her results have been compiled into an NDE Aftereffect brochure, which is published both on her website[35] and on the International Associations for Near Death Studies, Inc. website as well,[36] because her findings have been proven reliable.

Atwater and others have discovered that numerous psychological and physiological changes take place in the lives of

[32] "How Many NDEs Occur in the United States Every Day?" *Near Death Experience Research Foundation.* (D. Jeff, Editor) Accessed November 11, 2017. https://www.nderf.org/NDERF/Research/number_nde_usa.htm
[33] Gallup, G., & Proctor, W. *Adventures in Immortality: A Look Beyond the Threshhold of Death.* New York: McGraw-Hill, 1982.
[34] Atwater, P. *Near-Death Experiences: The Rest of the Story.* New York: MJF Books, 2011.
[35] Atwater, P. "Aftereffects of Near-Death States." Accessed November 7, 2017. http://pmhatwater.hypermart.net/page10/NDEAfter.html
[36] "Aftereffects of a Near-Death Experience." *International Association for Near Death Studies, Inc.* Accessed November 7, 2017. https://iands.org/aftereffects-of-near-death-states.html

NDErs, some of which I've already shared with you: the energy field around an NDEr that causes electrical snafus; an increased sensitivity to household chemicals; a name change because the NDEr feels like a different person; increased intuitive ability; and continued contact with high spiritual beings, among others.

It is fascinating to me that many of these modern-day revelations are recorded in age-old scripture, especially in the New Testament narratives attributed to Paul. After his STE, Paul continued to have contact and visionary experiences with high spiritual beings, and he spread the same messages as modern-day NDErs. The fact that these phenomena have remained both constant and common over two thousand years is evidence that both heaven is real and we never die.

As stated, one of the core characteristics of an NDE is that people describe seeing a Divine Light that they define as God, Jesus, Our Lady of Fátima, or the Supreme Being of the NDEr's belief system, whatever that might be. It doesn't even seem to require a belief system for the Divine Light to appear in an NDE. This is not suggesting there is more than one God; rather, it's saying the universal consciousness is the Super Natural Creator of every loved based belief system, no matter what it's called. I find it fascinating that Paul refers to the inclusion of other authorities, lords, and rulers in Colossians 1:16-17. It's also interesting to know that no cultural divides seems to be mentioned in Revelation 1:7: "Look! He comes with the clouds of heaven. And everyone will see him—even those who pierced him. And all the nations of the earth will weep because of him" (NLT).

Although I cannot personally verify this as being so, I can confirm without a doubt that we are spiritual beings of one divine body, so this is not beyond the omnipotent God I know. His abilities are limitless and not only is God real, but Jesus, the Holy Spirit, and other divine helpers are, too.

The passage Revelation 1:7 that conveys everyone will be welcomed in heaven, also says "all the nations of the earth." It doesn't say just some of us. This Supreme Being is love in its purest form—it radiates total, unconditional love and understanding—and the NDEr wants to stay forever. This experience has been reported so often that it has become a core characteristic of an NDE. Why? Because similar information repeated frequently becomes reliable.

Even if you haven't had an NDE, there are specific concepts and evidence that are shared in my experiences and other NDErs experiences that can lead us to trust in our hearts that heaven is real and we never die.

Consider also one of the psychological aftereffects of NDEs that NDErs love and accept others unconditionally without the usual societal constraints. Dr. Jeffrey Long performed a more in-depth study of this love phenomena in his book *God and the Afterlife.*[37] Dr. Long conducted a survey on 272 NDErs, focusing on whether the NDEr acquired specific information or awareness about love during their experience. Answers to the questions required an affirmative, a negative, or an uncertain response, but also required a narrative response with the answer.

The study results were evaluated two ways. First, Dr. Long noted that 58.1 percent of respondents answered that they felt

---

[37] Long, J., & Perry, P. *God and the Afterlife.* New York: HarperOne, 2016. E-book.

a higher sense of love during their experience. Then, the affirmative and uncertain narrative responses were analyzed. The results showed that the feeling of love, even though it was not given as a specific awareness or message to bring back, like the message I was given, love was significant to the personal experience of the NDEr. The narratives provided a new perspective, suggesting that 85% of NDErs experienced a feeling of love, a near 30% increase from the original answers. The sense of love was overwhelmingly significant in describing what and how they felt, even if they didn't receive the common message, like the one I received, that love is the only thing that matters.

Despite the shared features of a standard NDE, every person's experience is unique and fascinating. Despite how accounts may differ—how the person was taken up to heaven, what they saw, where they went, and whom they encountered—the existence of a supreme being and the message of love are consistent.

But rather than just the comfort in knowing that we never die, and love is what we will be enveloped in when we transition to heaven, the message gives us a lesson on how we should live. We should live with love in our hearts, because it is the energy of love that transforms darkness into light. Just think of your own life and how love and encouraging words could have made a situation better. A brilliant passage from the Bible that confirms this is Proverbs 15:4: "As a tree gives fruit, healing words give life, but dishonest words crush the spirit" (NCV).

There is not a single baby born who doesn't want to be loved. So, rather than tell a friend or loved one what they have done wrong, tell them what they're doing right. It is our human nature to want to please, so encouragement, positive uplifting words, and the ending of limited-mindedness makes us want to reach further.

We must always love and encourage others to be the best they can be, and look at life as an adventurous quest for golden nuggets of sacred knowledge. Every day we should look forward to what spiritual enlightenment we're going to encounter, and look forward to where these lessons lead us. Sometimes we get knocked down, and those are the moments we need to love ourselves the most.

Everything is surmountable. When you know what I know, or just have faith that God is with us, all the fears will melt away. You can shed those self-imposed restrictions and start becoming the beautiful, fantastic person you're supposed to be. You will be able to soar and learn to be the instrument of love that God wants you to be.

The message God gave me during my third NDE was that *love is the only thing that matters.* It echoed in me as my soul reentered my physical body. An overwhelming number of NDErs bring back this same message of love.

When this manuscript was complete, Jesus appeared with a proud countenance, a nod, and an awareness that I'd done a great job. I hope I've sufficiently conveyed the meaning behind the visions and other moments in my life that He provided me. We never die, He guides us through life unfailingly, and He loves us unconditionally. Our choices may change the course of our life, but certain events will occur no matter what direction our lives take. But more importantly, we all come home to the loving arms of our Creator when our earthly body remains behind.

Some people have expressed that they feel NDErs are blessed in some way. They say that this leaves them wanting an NDE, wondering why they haven't had one, too. I, however, do not believe we NDErs are the blessed ones. Jesus clarified this when Thomas wanted evidence that he was alive. Jesus gave him proof in John 20:29: "Then Jesus told him, 'You believe because you have seen me. Blessed are those who haven't seen me and believe anyway'" (NLT).

I will leave you, and that beautiful passage, as well as with this message that God gave me to bring back and share: Love is the only thing that matters.

REQUEST FROM THE AUTHOR

Writing this book has been an incredible privilege, and I hope my story has opened your mind to the spiritual world around us.

If you found my story has helped you in some way, please take a moment and go to the website where you made your purchase and search for my name. Searching for my name is the easiest way to find my book to leave a review. Please look up my book on Amazon, Barnes & Noble or Goodreads where you can scroll down to the rating section to choose the rating of choice.

Your ratings are paramount at telling interested buyers about the book's quality, and online book stores are more likely to promote what a book reader finds thought-provoking and helpful.

For larger orders, go to JanetTarantino.com for ordering instructions.

The next book currently in the works will cover my parent's journey toward the gates of heaven and what they shared with me while I cared for them. Because my parents knew of my NDE stories, it made them comfortable in communicating with me what they saw, sensed, or experienced in any way and what they described was incredible. The book will also include other people's NDE or spiritual accounts too.

ABOUT THE AUTHOR

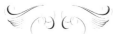

J ANET TARANTINO'S TRADITIONAL long-time career with one of the largest manufacturing companies of salty snack foods fostered her highly analytical, interpersonal, and teamwork skills, which propelled her to become a well-respected Network Coordinator organizing cost-effective ways to deliver products within a seven-state area.

Suddenly one summer, her life was changed forever when Janet, while on vacation, unexpectedly was involved in a severe car accident. What she experienced during the collision proved to her that our consciousness is not a function of the brain. Her reality crumbled when she found herself no longer in this earthly world, but instead looking back toward this one from an ethereal world in another dimension. Abruptly her life was different, but Heaven wasn't done with Janet. This unworldly experience set her up for an even more intense near-death experience that shook her to her core.

Now, after years of silence, she is ready to reveal why she knows we are never alone—God is real, we have a multitude of spiritual guidance available to help us like Jesus, the Holy

Spirit, Angels, and Angelic beings. She also states we plan what we want to learn, and we never die because our consciousness lives on into eternity. But more importantly, it's about how we should live. We should live knowing we can achieve our dreams; we can overcome adversity knowing God is with us, and most significantly we should live knowing love is the only thing that matters.

Janet's account of the supernatural powers of God supports our belief in heaven, the afterlife, and will give us faith and hope that we are unconditionally loved more than we know.

BIBLIOGRAPHY

"Aftereffects of a Near-Death Experience." *International Association for Near Death Studies, Inc.* Accessed November 7. 2017. https://iands.org/aftereffects-of-near-death-states.html

Alexander, E. M. *Proof of Heaven.* New York: Simon & Schuster, 2012.

Atwater, P. "Aftereffects of Near-Death States." Accessed November 7, 2017. http://pmhatwater.hypermart.net/page10/NDEAfter.html

Atwater, P. *Dying to Know You.* Faber, VA: Rainbow Ridge Book LLC, 2014. E-book.

Atwater, P. *Near-Death Experiences: The Rest of the Story.* New York: MJF Books, 2011.

Atwater, P. *The New Children and Near-Death Experiences.* Rochester, VM: Bear & Company, 2003. E-book.

Browne, S., & Harrison, L. *Book of Dreams.* New York: New American Library, 2003.

Browne, S., & Harrison, L. *Visits from the Afterlife.* New York: New American Library, 2003. E-book.

Burpo, T., & Vincent, L. *Heaven is for Real* (Special Movie Edition ed.). Nashville: W Publishing Group, 2003.

"Child Development Tracker, Language." PBS. Accessed November 7, 2017. http://www.pbs.org/parents/childdevelopmenttracker/one/language.html

"Dr. Eben Alexander III MD." *Eben Alexander.* Accessed November 8, 2017. http://ebenalexander.com/about/

"Dr. Mary Neal - Raised from the dead Part2 Converging Zone with Robert Ricciardelli." YouTube video, 30:51. Accessed June 20, 2014. https://www.youtube.com/watch?v=ULsl92H-Noc

Dunwell, T., *Living Works Studio,* Accessed March 6, 2018. http://livingworksstudio.com

Gallup, G., & Proctor, W. *Adventures in Immortality: A Look Beyond the Threshhold of Death.* New York: McGraw-Hill, 1982.

Greyson, B. "Near-Death Experiences." In *Varieties of Anomalous Experience.* 2nd ed. Edited by S. J. Lynn, et al. Washington, DC: American Psychological Association, 2014.

Hinn, B. *Good Morning Holy Spirit.* Nashville: Thomas Nelson, Inc, 1997. E-book.

Hinn, B. *He Touched Me: Benny Hinn an Autobiography.* Nashville: Thomas Nelson, Inc., 1999.

"How Many NDEs Occur in the United States Every Day?" *Near Death Experience Research Foundation.* (D. Jeff, Editor) Accessed November 11, 2017. https://www.nderf.org/NDERF/Research/number_nde_usa.htm

Kramarik, A., & Kramarik, F. *Akiane: Her Life, Her Art, Her Poetry.* Nashville: Thomas Nelson, 2006.

Kramarik. Art Akiane LLC. *Prince of Peace.* Accessed November 8, 2017. https://akiane.com/product/prince-of-peace/

Long, J., & Perry, P. *God and the Afterlife.* New York: HarperOne, 2016. E-book.

Neal, Mary C. *To Heaven and Back.* New York: WaterBook Multnomah, 2012. E-book.

Moody, R. *Life After Life.* New York: HarperCollins Publishers, 2015.

Myss, C. *Entering the Castle.* New York: Free Press, 2007.

"Myoclonus Information Page." *NIH National Institute of Neurological Disorders and Stroke.* Accessed November 14, 2017. http://www.ninds.nih.gov/Disorders/All-Disorders/Myoclonus-Information-Page

Romano, David. "When Tomorrow Starts Without Me." In Canfield, J., Hansen, M., & Kirberger, K. *Chicken Soup for the Soul on Tough Stuff.* Cos Cob, Connecticut: Chicken Soup for the Soul Publishing, 2012.

Rouse, M. "Quantum Theory." *Whatls.* Accessed February 6, 2018. http://whatis.techtarget.com/definition/quantum-theory

Wallace, R. dir. *Heaven is for Real.* 2014. Culver City, CA: Sony Pictures. DVD.

Made in the USA
Columbia, SC
17 May 2022